fragments

fragments

my path through the 20th century

kit tremaine

Blue Dolphin Publishing
1992

For information, address:
Blue Dolphin Publishing, Inc.
P.O. Box 1908
Nevada City, CA 95959

ISBN: 0-931892-73-2

Library of Congress Cataloging-in-Publication Data

Tremaine, Kit, 1907-
    Fragments : my path through the 20th century /
    Kit Tremaine.
        p.   cm.
    ISBN 0-931892-73-2 : $12.95
    1. Tremaine, Kit, 1907- . 2. Socialites—United States—
Biography.   3. Women political activists—Unites States—
Biography.   4. Women philanthropists—United States—
Biography.   I. Title.
CT275.T8686A3 1991
973.92'092—dc20
[B]   91-38221
                                                              CIP

Printed in the United States of America by
Blue Dolphin Press, Inc., Grass Valley, California

9   8   7   6   5   4   3   2   1

This book is dedicated
to my three children
Teddy, Diana, and Katy
with love and appreciation
for the many lessons they taught me

Special thanks to my editors—Marianne Partridge,
former editor of the *Village Voice*
and currently editor of *The Santa Barbara Independent*,
Steve Diamond, author and friend,
and novelist Gayle Stone,
invaluable in countless ways.

Table of Contents

Introduction

I HAVE LIVED IN MANY HOUSES. Some were large and elaborate, some small and simple. A few were rented, others were built and owned by my husband and myself. One was designed and built by a world-famous architect and became a mecca for people from many parts of the world.

I went yesterday to visit an old friend who is dying and was reminded of the long ago early morning when hearing the doorbell ring, I looked to see my friend, who was then working for me as my butler, standing at the door talking with a young couple in French. He was telling them that he would ask me if it would be convenient for them to see the house as they had not written ahead. My friend, a black man, had grown up on a farm in Louisiana, and although virtually illiterate, had spoken French all his life.

That house in Santa Barbara was designed and built for us by the architect Richard Neutra, and was considered by many critics to be the best thing he had done up to that time. It was built of native stone and glass with floors of terrazzo, and it was interesting to watch the

stone masons handling the stone during building. They
sat on the ground with the stone between their legs,
chipping patiently away with a wedge-like instrument
as in the time of Christ, tiny bits flaking away until the
stone had reached the desired shape. All this to form the
dramatic and quite formal structure that was the finished
product.

Each house has left me memories, not only the
houses themselves, but the landscapes they occupied,
the views I saw from their windows, the life I lived in
them, and, most of all, the people I shared them with.

So I shall write about my life in terms of where and
how I have lived, and with whom. A friend suggested to
me not long ago that I could be described as a woman
who has progressed from socialite to political activist to
spiritual seeker. It sounds rather grandiose, but it does
have a ring of truth.

As everyone's life is, mine too has been a journey of
transformation: if nothing else, from struggling to become an adult after coping with being born into a
wealthy family and then enduring childhood. It is hard
to grow up.

And I believe that I started to grow up on that day
in late October, 1968, when I drove for the last time
down the long winding driveway through the unspoiled
oak forest, the setting for the house I had lived in for
thirty years. I had been for all of my life the observer. It
was as if I had always stood behind the curtain, on stage,
yet not a part of the cast, and now the curtain was about
to go up and I was ready for it.

CHAPTER ONE

The Atchafalaya

The Earth whirls
I stand
in the middle
watching

THE ATCHAFALAYA RIVER MEANDERS placidly through the southwestern part of Louisiana where I was born in the early part of the twentieth century. I was born under a money tree, and for all of my life I have had only to shake it gently to have a rain of glittering gold shower down around me.

My money tree was a gaunt, virtually leafless water cypress and with its fellows stood in the placid brown waters of Louisiana's Atchafalaya Bayou. Their gnarled and exposed roots stood firmly in the water, and twisting around and through them cottonmouth snakes and catfish shared their lives with a myriad of life forms indigenous to the warm, brackish waters. As this sleepy river meanders through the southwestern part of Louisiana, the mighty Mississippi has been trying for years to join it. And when it does succeed, and surely it will, the face

11

of the land will be altered forever and death and destruc-
tion will result. The fierce torrent from the larger river
will force the Atchafalaya from its banks, and the rich
and pleasant land that is now the Atchafalaya Basin will
be deep underwater. Thousands of people might die—
animals, reptiles, the crops in the ground, the oil and
other minerals beneath the ground, all will be flooded
out, and it will be many years before nature can restore
her gifts to Louisiana.

It is Cajun country, though we had no claim to that
heritage. The Cajuns were the direct descendants of the
French Canadians who had, after being forced out of
Nova Scotia by the British, wandered the country until
they came to the warm and pleasant land of Louisiana.
This suited the settlers and there they stayed to found
their music-loving, food-loving, French-speaking culture. The name they are known by is a corruption of a
longer one, Acadian, the province of Canada they had
left being known as Acadia. Henry Wadsworth Longfel-
low, the nineteenth-century poet, wrote his long narra-
tive poem, *Evangeline*, about the arduous trek of the
Cajuns from the rocky shores of Nova Scotia to the
brackish bayous of southwest Louisiana, and there they
live to this day, cooking, eating, singing, making music,
while fishing and trapping in the fecund waters of their
chosen home.

The Cajuns brought a new culture to the land, an
enriching culture that has greatly nourished the countryside in many ways. Strangely, it is only now, just
coming out of the eighties into the nineties, that the
Cajuns have become immensely popular. Cajun cook-

ing, Cajun music, Cajun celebrations . . . everything Cajun is popular. It used to be that there was no particular notice paid to them; they were just there in southern Louisiana and blackened redfish had never been heard of, but it is different now.

To this pleasant land came my grandfather, Frank Bennett Williams, a tall, spare man, who had come to Louisiana from Alabama after the Civil War. His mother was a widowed school teacher with a son and two daughters to raise in an impoverished land, and my grandfather, being the sole breadwinner in his family, chose to seek his fortune in Louisiana. He found work there with one of the railroads and as time went on he married and established his own family. I have heard two stories concerning his career, one that he was a conductor on a train, the other that he came as a surveyor. Both are true, and he was farsighted enough to buy cheap swamp land with his earnings, mile after mile of water with gaunt cypress trees growing in brackish brown water. Later, "F.B.," as he was called, harvested millions of board feet of cypress and his fortune grew as his trees disappeared. Two of my close childhood friends insisted always that my grandfather had cheated their fathers out of much land, and perhaps he had. That he was successful is attested to by the fact that he became one of the state's most prominent citizens, as well as one of its wealthiest.

One of my grandfather's half-dozen lumber mills was situated in the little village of Patterson, Louisiana, and it was there that we lived, my parents, my older brother, and I, for the first few years of my life before

moving into New Orleans, which at that time was
several hours away by train but now two or three hours
away by car over smooth freeways.

Our house in the country where I was born was
square, built in the way of the plantation dwellings of
the time. The main rooms were on the second floor. The
ground floor held the servants' rooms and storage areas.
Outdoors, a broad staircase led up to the front door from
the ground below. There were probably three or four
bedrooms, a living room, dining room, and the kitchens
in the back. I remember my astonishment when I first
saw a kitchen built in the front of a house. I thought it
a very good idea, particularly in the city, where privacy
was a consideration. But ours looked out on the back
yard, with chickens scratching in the dust. I could see
my grandparents' house from ours, beyond the small
vine-covered screened house where the night watchman
slept the night away. Theirs was a large, rambling, two-
story Victorian house, perfectly suited to the youthful
middle-aged man who was raising a family in it while
building an empire around the state.

My brother and I called our grandparents Mere and
Pere in the French manner. The custom probably had
begun as Grandmere and Grandpere, but we had
dropped the first part so that they were always Mere and
Pere to us. I don't have many clear recollections of those
earliest years, mainly falling off my bicycle and being
replaced by a servant and having my black knee protec-
tors straightened once again, an attempt at keeping my
permanently scabbed knees clean.

My brother was two years older than I and seemed to be everyone's favorite child. I am sure this explains my competitive drive in certain areas, noticeably in intellectual ones. I had a real desire to be out from under his shadow and to leave behind me achievements which might make my mother reconsider her somewhat low opinion of my intellect. Incidentally, I have done this and I take pleasure in knowing it. I laugh when I think that when I was told I was to be given an honorary doctorate, my first thought was of my mother and what I thought was, "That would show her. Laurence never had that distinction bestowed on him." Of course, both my mother and Laurence had passed on by that time, but still the thought came to me.

I occupied the nursery of that house, a large sunny room, with my brother and our nurse, a tall, dignified mulatto woman named Julia. Julia spoke fluent French, as did many people in Louisiana, and according to my mother was wildly admired by men in France and Italy during the two years we spent in Europe.

My mother used to say she felt sorry for me when I was little as Julia showed so plainly her preference for my brother, but the preference I remember yearning for was not Julia's but my mother's. I longed to be her favorite child, but that was not to be my role in the family.

My brother Laurence, and Fraulein, our governess who came after Julia, both contracted typhoid fever from contaminated milk on a trip into New Orleans, and many months passed with trained nurses living in the house with us. I remember one breakfast when one of them sat next to me, and to persuade me to eat my hominy grits, she drew a small canyon in the pile of grits, put butter into it telling me it was the Panama Canal. I was about five, but old enough to think she was very tiresome.

**

Southwest Louisiana is fairly flat, and to some it might be considered uninteresting. To me, however, it is a land of quiet beauty, a bit stark, but I respond to that in other landscapes too. The swamps, where those two-hundred-or-more-year-old cypress trees reached down their probing roots into the dark waters and found their anchor among nests of water snakes and the twisted root system of the hyacinths, those trees are hauntingly beautiful and I've never quite gotten my fill of them. Every now and then I think of returning to Louisiana once more just to see the swamps and the mighty Mississippi River. It is a place where one can imagine ghosts flitting among gaunt cypress trunks, beings other than ourselves, light beings perhaps, or even wispy threads of smoke winding a tenuous way through a haunting scene. At certain times of the year the Atchafalaya River is choked with a solid mass of greenery interspersed with the pale lavender blossoms of the water hyacinth. These fragile looking flowers had been brought back from a long past trip to China by a New Orleans woman who had seen them there and had fallen in love with their delicate beauty. She never dreamed that years afterwards they would be a hazard to navigation in the tideless bayous of Louisiana.

The house where I was born stood on a large piece of land that sloped down to the river, although the river itself was not visible from the houses—my grandparents' or ours. There were barns and other buildings clustered around the dwellings, and between the houses and the bayou lay pastures for grazing animals, groves of ancient live oak trees, and my favorite location, a pig pen with its occupants wallowing contentedly in rich, black mud. I have a great appreciation for pigs, while holding an irrational fear of bears. (Perhaps I had a bad bear experience in a former lifetime.) To stand on the lower railing of the pig pen fence, leaning as far over as I dared, was to me a perfect way to pass the time. My brother and Fraulein didn't share my pig-love, and it was a rare occasion when I could persuade them to take the detour down Piggy Lane through the fields to the pigs.

The grounds surrounding our houses were enclosed by a wrought-iron fence which I believe still stands. Between them was a small, screened house, almost entirely covered with sweet-smelling vines, jasmine, honeysuckle, and dark green shrubs heavy with the almost overpowering scent of sweet olive blossoms. This little house was where our night watchman spent his nights, either reading by a tiny lamp, or just as likely, snoozing the night away. I liked him very much and pestered him often for stories of which he had an unending store. He was called Bat by the family, and I have wondered often if it was because of the fact that he was a night watchman, therefore presumably able to see in the dark, or if perhaps his name actually was Bat. Alas, there is no one left alive to tell me. It was a slight shock for me to realize recently that now, at eighty-four, I am the oldest member of my family, the matriarch, and as I never took much interest in family history when it was being offered to me, I really know little about the past.

There were quite a few out-buildings connected with the houses, a small structure housing an ice-making machine, a bowling alley, wood shed, cool rooms where fruits and vegetables could be kept fresh—this was long before refrigeration had been thought of—and a large cistern on long legs that kept it high off the ground. The cistern caught the rainwater which served as drinking water as well as every other use. There was a carriage house already partially converted into a garage in the time I write about, and there were various others of which I have no particular memory.

One hot afternoon I became temporarily attached to the pipe on the outside of the icehouse when, passing it, I paused to lick off the ice that had collected on the pipe. My tongue stuck to the pipe, and there I stood, tears streaming down my face, unable to move and causing great concern to my brother and our two cousins. One of them ran into the house for help and brought back one of the maids who sized up the situation and immediately ran inside to fetch a pitcher of warm water which she then poured carefully over my tongue until the ice melted sufficiently to free me.

I am reminded of another hot afternoon when I stood in front of the house in the sunshine watching with unbelieving eyes as a rain shower was falling on the far side of the road. "The devil's fighting with his wife because she put too much salt in the soup," one of the servants told me.

***

My grandfather owned what was probably the only Mercedes automobile in Louisiana at the time, certainly it was the first. This red beauty was housed in the very center of the gleaming floor of the dual-purpose carriage house that had already begun its partial transformation into a garage. There was a large hay loft above, and we children spent many happy hours up there jumping and rolling around in the sweet-smelling piles of hay.

My grandparents' dwelling was a two-story Victorian mansion, at least to my childhood eyes it was a mansion. A multi-colored bead curtain divided the dining room from the living room, and it, of course, fascinated me. Equally fascinating was the gaudy parrot whose cage was generally placed close enough to the curtain for it to reach through the bars and tweak gently at the colorful beads. This produced a small tinkling sound, as interesting to me as the beads and the bird.

This large house had a series of halls and passages. Trying to recreate it leads me to wondering at what early point in their lives my grandparents decided to sleep in separate rooms as they were already doing at the time my memory walks me through their house. This was unusual in that era. We all know how impossible it is to imagine our forebears' lives. Try to picture your parents enjoying sex. Enjoying sex! Surely they didn't do that! At least not in that era!

My grandfather slept in an enormous mahogany folding bed. It was a feather bed, an extraordinary object that must surely have been custom made. When I was around ten or twelve years old, and my grandparents no longer lived in the country, I had occasion to spend the night in that very bed. My brother and I were visiting my uncle and aunt who were living there, and we had been given adjoining rooms. It was my fate to have this huge feather bed, and it frightened me a little as it soon occurred to me that the bed might spring up against the wall, and I would be smothered with no one to hear my cries.

It was a night of dense fog, a common occurrence in Louisiana, especially near a river, and I had recently been reading Dracula. Between staring fixedly at the window, sure that the fog curling in underneath the screen was the vampire himself, and juggling desperate decisions related to possible action in the event that the bed suddenly left the floor for its daytime anchorage against the wall, I spent a miserable night.

When we lived in the country, my brother Laurence and I had been given a stylish looking little cart, called for some reason a "governess cart." For us it was appropriately named, as it was our governess who accompanied us on our afternoon expeditions, and it was she who held the reins as we proceeded along the dusty country roads. The gift of the cart included a fat and placid brown Shetland pony to whom we gave the inspired name of

Thursday, that having been the day of the week on which he had come into our lives. As the grownup, Fraulein had control over our destination, and if I wanted to go to see the pigs, as I always did, it was up to me to coax her, and also my brother, to agree to a side trip down Piggy Lane. This tree-shaded lane took us not only to the pigpen, but if we followed it all the way we could end up right at the edge of the bayou and maybe catch a glimpse of an alligator. As neither my brother nor Fraulein shared my enthusiasm for pigs, I never had enough time to watch them, gloating over their lush, sensuous beauty, their snuffling noises, their smells, and their ecstasy as they wallowed in the mud. Both of my companions preferred a smart trot down the main road, dirt, of course, as all roads were at that time, and generally we would end up doing just that. To this day if I am lucky enough to find myself at a country fair, which doesn't happen too often, I head straight for the swine section where once again I can gaze in contemplative delight at my porcine friends.

The Atchafalaya had, and I am sure still has, its share of snakes and alligators. My aunt, mother of my two cousins, once told me of going out and shooing the alligators from the back yard with a dishcloth, shouting alarms all the while, whenever one would come lumbering up from the water to chase one of the chickens squawking about the place. In retrospect I feel that I really would have loved seeing that, but at the same time I would have been terrified.

The atmosphere at Idlewild, the name of our cousins' home, was far more relaxed than at our house on the other side of town. There were no servants, and both Auntee and Uncle Ned were easy-going souls. My cousin Teddy was a delicate child, severely afflicted with croup, and around his slender, childish neck he wore a necklace of what appeared to be enormous amber beads. Auntee assured us these would both ward off and cure his malady, and who is to say that they didn't? I know that if folk medicine hadn't proven successful over the years, it long since would have disappeared from our midst, instead of which, its influence is stronger now than ever before and modern medicine's debt to it is openly acknowledged.

Although I stopped trying to compete with the boys as we got older, a few specific memories remain with me. With the exception of Teddy, a year or so younger than me, my brother Laurence, and Steve, Teddy's older brother, naturally had more skills and more strength than I did. I never succeeded, for example, in climbing what seemed to my eyes an enormous corrugated iron pipe, but the boys scrambled up its slippery sides with ease. This challenging object stood in the unkempt front yard at Idlewild, so naturally we knew it had been put there for our entertainment. I never made it, though I tried. I puffed and panted as far up its slippery sides as I could until the inevitable happened and down I would go.

I never succeeded in blowing the large black rubber horn on my grandfather's bright red Mercedes either, so it was no wonder that as I got to be around seven years old I yearned to be turned into a boy. In New Orleans, there was a druggist who assured me that he had the formula for such a transformation. What I had to do, he explained, was to kiss my elbow and then he would give me the magic prescription that would immediately and magically turn me into a boy. It wasn't for lack of trying that I never succeeded. I tried and tried, but, as you will discover for yourself, unless you are double or triple jointed, to kiss your elbow is not something that many can do.

To be a boy, I reasoned, would give me some of the magic in my mother's eyes that my brother already had, and surely she would love me then. Once Auntie Belle, my great-aunt, offered to take me downtown dressed in a boy's suit and to introduce me as her little nephew. I loved the idea, and was told that I could wear one of my brother's outgrown sailor suits. I was pretty proud of myself and walked along Canal Street, I remember, not even holding my aunt's hand. In spite of her warnings that little boys were not expected to curtsy on meeting a grownup, I was so used to this custom that I kept forgetting and she kept laughing, until finally we had to give it up and confess that I wasn't really little Tommy Williams but in fact myself, Kit Williams.

CHAPTER TWO

Growing Up In New Orleans

being a child
so soon over . . .
the tenderness

MY MOTHER USED TO SAY with a straight face that, in the weeks preceding my birth, she was so large that it was impossible for her to climb a flight of stairs unless someone pushed her from behind. This could well have been true as I weighed just under eleven pounds. Since she was rather short, she probably was overbalanced. Perhaps I over-balanced her all during my life, which might explain, in part, why she always tended to put me down.

My mother liked to tell a story concerning me at an early age when I apparently was being so horrible to my older brother that my father finally said, "Alright Laurence, you've taken enough, you can go ahead and hit her." Whereupon Laurence hit me so hard that he knocked me flat on the ground.

Considering that I must have been all of four or five years old at that time, this seems like rather harsh treatment for a small girl. My mother always told this story with relish, ending with a definite note of triumph in her voice as she said: "And then Laurence walked up to you and swung so hard he knocked you down."

By now I have had my own struggles with my own children and I am aware of the impossibility of seeing any situation through another's eyes. Still I have carried the hurt of my mother's preference for my brother all during my life. I remember once when she and I and a friend were discussing preferences for one's children, my mother remarked smugly that she had been lucky, she had borne only two children, one of each sex, so that there had never been a need for her to have a preference. "Don't you believe it!" I said, and wondered if she had any idea of what I was really saying.

Years later, while visiting my mother in New Orleans, we went together to a cocktail party. Just before leaving I was chatting with a lifelong friend, and in answer to something he said I responded with a remark that displeased her. My mother and I left shortly thereafter, and we were hardly seated in the back seat of her car before she began to castigate me. I reminded her that I was about to be forty years old (a lifetime, two lifetimes ago, as I am today eighty-three years old), that I had three children, had been married twice, and had done many things of which she would not approve, but that it was my life and that I must live it as I thought best.

"You surely can't expect to tell me for the rest of my life how I should conduct myself. I have to live my life, just as you do yours." This had an effect on my mother and she never again spoke to me in that tone of righteous parent to incorrigible child. Would that I could say the same in my relations with my own children.

I once knew a woman who so despised herself that this feeling extended into everything about her, her husband and her children, most especially her children who were never allowed to express an opinion on even the slightest matter. I recall one Sunday when we were having lunch with this family and the conversation turned on the family's plans for the summer. Someone voiced a suggestion whereupon the middle boy agreed enthusiastically, saying how much he loved the idea. His mother turned angrily on him, telling him to be quiet, that nobody had asked his opinion on anything.

***

We were never a close family in the sense of togetherness. We didn't go on picnics or to the movies together: we rarely even ate together when my brother and I were children. The grownups lived their lives and we lived ours. It was, in fact, in the nature of a treat to have dinner with our parents rather than earlier in the evening with our governess. Laurence and I sat on one side of the table with Mademoiselle on the other, and our mother and father at each end.

On the nights when we had river shrimp, a seasonal delicacy and a delight to eat, I would rush through my serving, reach over to my brother's plate and treat myself to as big a handful as I could snatch before the expected complaint and the reprimand that inevitably followed. The shrimp were tiny, served on beds of crushed ice.

They were not shelled before being cooked, so had to be shelled at the dinner table. I was quick and gobbled mine down long before Laurence had made much of a dent in his supply. "Mother, Kit's eating my shrimp again!" was a cry often heard on shrimp nights.

Later, during the years when Laurence and I were at boarding schools in the East, on our first night home for vacation, my mother generally gave us the things we most liked to eat for dinner. My favorite menu consisted of river shrimp as a first course, followed by fried chicken with mashed potatoes and fresh peas, and then to cap it off, chocolate ice cream with marshmallow sauce. To this day, I prefer that dessert to any other.

In our early childhood days, my brother and I were tutored at home by an Austrian governess until World War I broke out, when, for reasons having to do with patriotism I assume, she was replaced by a Mademoiselle. We learned quite a lot with Fraulein, however. I was reading by the time I was four, and fairly competently, in both English and German. We learned little bits and pieces of the German language during those years, but later were tutored in French, a language also taught in the schools. French has proven to be very useful to me all during my life as I have found that in many places I have travelled where English is not spoken, French often is.

When I wasn't in the house with Fraulein, I was outside, perhaps struggling to learn to ride my brother's outgrown bicycle, trying to balance myself when I had to slow down, generally falling off when stopping, and being picked up by the chauffeur or some other patient soul. I was all right if I managed to bring my steed close enough to the stairs leading up to the front porch, as then it was easy to disembark with one foot on a stair. I often had to be rescued by someone, picked up, dusted off and have the black knee pads I was wearing checked to be sure they were in place, and even so my knees wore permanent scabs. Because of this caring atmosphere I grew to think of the various servants as my best friends. Skates and bikes and gravel driveways aren't the most compatible of companions, but I couldn't see letting my brother do all of those things and not try to keep up with him, if not indeed surpass him. It sounds ridiculous, I know, but a few years ago when I was told that I was to be awarded an honorary doctorate, my first and entirely involuntary thought was, "That would show her!" I know that you can guess who "her" was. And this when I was in my seventies!

Actually it wasn't my brother I wanted to impress. It was my mother's love and approval I was always hoping for. As she seemed always to approve of my brother, it followed that I must try to outdo him.

***

I wonder how many of us look back on childhood as a happy time? Often I hear others speak of it that way, but for myself I only seem to remember its darker aspects. As an example, I don't remember ever having had a birthday party. Not one in all my childhood, although I am certain there must have been some.

Thinking of parties and birthday cakes, I have a clear recollection of going into my brother's room one spring afternoon where he lay recuperating from typhoid, which had struck both Laurence and Fraulein. We still lived in the small village of Patterson where one of my grandfather's mills was situated, but Lawrence's typhoid had been picked up in New Orleans from contaminated milk. Our mother was sitting by his bed reading to him as I rushed in excitedly, saying I had just been in the kitchen and had seen an enormous chocolate cake that we were going to have for dessert. I'd hardly spoken the words when Laurence burst into tears. My mother turned to me angrily, demanding to know how I could do such a thing to poor Laurence who, because of his illness, was on a strict diet and unable to eat sweets. At the tender age of five, diets were not a big part of my life, and I was shocked to be sent from the room, evidently not being considered worthy of being in the same room with them.

Cooks and maids and butlers are the ones who gave me love when I was growing up. Once when I was talking with a psychiatrist and recounting my—what seemed to me—loveless life, he asked me who it was that had loved me, as he felt there were qualities in me that told him I had been loved. Without a moment's hesitation I told him about Mrs. Bird. Mrs. Alexandrine Bird was a remarkable woman who came to live in our house and work for us when I was around nine years old.

She was originally hired by my mother to be a seamstress, and that she did well, but it was only one of her roles in our lives. Living as we did in the South, most of our help was black and went to their own homes and families at night. But Mrs. Bird was not black, and she had no house and no family, so we became her family, most particularly me. She had raised, single-handedly, six sons. The father of the boys had deserted his family, and she sent all of them through college with the help of a church institution where they had grown up.

I was the little girl Mrs. Bird had always wanted but never had. I became her little girl. For example, when one of my friends began to develop breasts and actually wore a bra, I wanted desperately to have one too, in spite of the fact that I didn't have anything to make me eligible for one. Although my mother said no, very firmly, Mrs. Bird said not to worry and made me one. It was pink and trimmed with tiny rosebuds and pink satin bows. The bra was a secret from my mother, of course, and I was the proudest girl in the neighborhood.

Mrs. Bird was as homely a woman as could be found. I can see her now, all these years later, as clearly as if it were last week. She was rather spare in body and bent a bit as she walked. She limped slightly from years of hard work and arthritis. She wore her sparse brown-gray hair in a knot on her neck and her nose was too big for her face. My mother thought it funny that Mrs. Bird worried about her looks when she was so homely anyway. To have a new dress was a rare event for Mrs. Bird, and when it was time to get one, she would always consult my mother for her advice. At these times my mother invariably had a comment about her looks.

"Funny," said my mother confidentially, "when you are as ugly as Bird, what difference does it make what you wear?" But to Mrs. Bird it made a difference, and when one of her sons was coming to visit her, to take her out to dinner, perhaps, or to a movie, like any other woman she wanted to be a credit to him.

I am not sure what became of those six men. My recollection is that they all did well for themselves. One joined the Merchant Marine, and small gifts would come to Bird from many parts of the world. I do know that each one of them honored their mother and gave her respect and love.

As I write of the bitterness I had towards my mother, I must also write of her many charms and talents. She was rather small, had naturally wavy brown hair and greenish-hazel eyes. She leaned toward floral prints in summer clothes, small perky hats, often with flower trim, and although she would have been termed "well dressed," her taste was never my own. Her name was Phoebe, Phoebe Nixon in fact, and as I never liked the name, I was grateful that she hadn't given it to me. Being as I am a lifelong politically radical thinker, I hastened always to assure anyone who needed to know my mother's maiden name that we were not related to the Nixon who subsequently became president.

One of my clearest recollections of my mother was when she was dressing one night for a costume party. She wore a pale green dress of a thin cotton fabric. It fell around her knees in a ragged, uneven hem and although the sleeves were nonexistent, a few ragged pieces of light green fell over her bare upper arms. Her brown hair hung loose down her back, and I see myself again, standing by her dressing table watching as she twines grapes into her hair. My mother became, at that instant, the epitome of all that a small girl could wish to be. She was the unattainable object, as she always was in some obscure way.

My mother was the youngest of four children. Her father had died while still a young lawyer, leaving behind his red-haired wife and four small children. Grandmother was a resourceful and extremely intelligent woman, and having a large house and several in help, she took in boarders and ran a Montessori-type school as well that was funded by wealthy friends. She was not only its administrator, but its headmistress as well, and taught English literature in her spare time.

There was not much money for the family when my mother was growing up. My impression is that they were always dependent on more affluent relatives for treats, such as performances at the French Opera House and the like. My mother described how they, her mother and her three siblings, would be offered a box at the opera by a wealthy relative, and how eagerly she waited with the other children for the carriage to come clopping up the driveway to their front door to take them away for the evening's entertainment. As a consequence, she knew opera backwards and forwards, and was often heard humming familiar arias.

I also recall her telling me that when she was around four or five, every morning when she came down to the breakfast table Grandmother would say to her, "Phoebe, have you cleaned your teeth this morning?" She would reply that she had not, whereupon she was sent back upstairs to clean her teeth. I asked her why she didn't just clean them and so avoid the trip upstairs, and her reply was that she was always hoping that her mother would forget to ask her and that then she would have won. It clearly was a contest of wills. It makes me wonder how often I did similar things in "combat" with my mother or my children. Looking back on it, I see that I found it hard to think of my mother being so playful, and it makes me stop and rethink her nature.

Had she not been so charming herself, my mother would have been a cold person. It was impossible for her to receive graciously—whether it was an abstraction, such as a compliment, or a material gift. She enjoyed playing Lady Bountiful. I suppose that this trait stemmed from the fact that in her youth she been so much on the receiving. She had many devoted friends, however, and never lacked for loyalty from those who worked for her. I came to believe that my mother was charming to everyone but her daughter.

One reason, perhaps, was that unlike her own life, mine had begun with riches to grant my every desire. This was so different from her own that I thought she resented the contrast between her youth and mine. When my mother was growing up she and her family were dependent on wealthier relatives for favors, and I think this inclined her towards being very materialistic, which for me defined her nature.

I was blessed with a great deal, being young, pretty, rich and intelligent, although this last was an area that my mother liked to deny, loudly and often. "Billy always says that the worst investment he ever made was the money he spent on Kit's education. She's very pretty," my mother would continue, gazing fondly at me, her eyes twinkling, "but not really very bright."

There were two things wrong with this pronouncement. The first was that my father actually adored me—a fact by the way which caused me considerable guilt later on—so that it wasn't likely that he actually said those words. It was far more likely that my mother invented it herself as yet another little way of putting me down. The second was that I was, and am, intelligent, and school never presented me with problems.

I now believe that my mother didn't want me to be smart for two reasons: the first was that she so loved my older brother, Laurence, also blessed with an excellent mind, that I wasn't to be allowed to encroach on his accomplishments. The other reason, however, may well have been the important one, as she repeated it to me in different ways over the years. A girl, a woman, was never supposed to be considered—or "found out" would be another way of putting it—to be smarter, more proficient at golf, tennis, bridge, or in fact, anything, than a man. There was no doubt that she was wedded to this idea. Perhaps it was because we lived in New Orleans, the Deep South, where women always had to keep their places, ideally a few paces behind their men, certainly not out in front in any way. I hope this is no longer the popularly held view of the man/woman relationship in the South, but it wouldn't surprise me if it still is prevalent to this day.

While all of the above is true, my mother was simultaneously a pretty advanced female for her time. She actually smoked in public, drove a car until she had an accident that traumatized her so badly that she never drove again, and worked on political committees, she did, in fact, all kinds of things which probably were ahead of her time, while retaining the values that she had been been taught as a child. I wonder now in retrospect, all these many years later, what she would have thought about the person I have become?

I have come to believe that we would be better off to discard the teachings we received as children. Not the values, necessarily, but the rules we were taught. Integrity, honesty, compassion—these qualities are timeless and never to be ignored, but a great deal of what we learned as children is irrelevant to our lives. Victorian virtues were still being extolled when I was born in the first decade of this century. I maintain that we must think for ourselves, and if we find ourselves out of step with our peers, it may be that it is we who are right, and our peers who live with outmoded values.

I remember a young mother telling me a few years ago that her small son didn't want to do the things she had done at his age or accept the values she lived by. I said that what she had done, or thought, was probably entirely irrelevant to her child's life. He was being a child now, not ten years ago: a different world, different ideas, prevailed at this time, and his life would be lived in a very different atmosphere than her's had been.

It is hard to realize that it doesn't work to tell a child, or anyone else, that they must do as you say simply because you say it. My husband used to tell our children just that, and it never worked. And indeed, why should it?

***

A wonderful thing happened when I was about eight years old. A family from Vicksburg, Mississippi, bought the large house next door to ours. When they moved in, I was discovered that there were seven children in the family. The one about in the middle of the group became my special friend, and the boy who was eleven or twelve became the love object in my life at the time.

Miss Ella was my friend's name, pronounced as one word, Missella. I spent countless hours sitting on the sidewalk with Missella and other little girls playing endless games of jacks when we weren't climbing up among the sharply pungent branches of the camphor trees. What bliss, I thought, to live in such a household.

The family from Mississippi was our neighbor for only a few years, and when they returned to their home state I was invited to visit. I was put on the train at our end of the trip, in the big, sooty station at the end of New Orleans' Canal Street, and met at the other end by Missella and an older member of the family. I am a bit ashamed to confess that my chief memory of the voyage was my costume. I wore an extremely sophisticated and, in my eyes, grown up outfit. I feel sure that I had a wonderful time with my friends on my first solo trip away from home, but what I remember is the pleated navy blue and green tartan skirt I wore, the pristine white shirt with the little round collar under the navy blue blazer with—most glorious of all glories—brass buttons!

One of my playmates was a boy around my brother's age. This was Henry, the grandson of our cook. Generally, in the South at that time, the help left after dinner to go to their own homes, returning to work the following morning. On moving to New Orleans from the country, we rented a house so we could decide what part of the city we would settle in before buying. This house was in New Orleans' Garden District and boasted a separate servants' quarters. Our cook had requested permission of my mother to bring her little grandson to New Orleans from the country so that he could go to a better school than would have been available to him in the small town where he lived with his family. Everyone was pleased with this arrangement, including, of course, my brother and myself as here was someone who always would be around as a playmate.

Soon I noticed something different about the manner in which Henry was treated. When we came in the house, Henry was allowed only in the kitchen, pantry, or possibly the dining room, never in the living room, and certainly not upstairs. Those hideous dark red velvet curtains that hung in the living room and that totally obscured any light from outside, were never to be seen by Henry. His aesthetic sense would never be jarred by those curtains, nor was the heavily-carved and highly polished furniture available to him.

When I asked my mother why this was so, I did not feel satisfied with her answers, couched in vague terms and relating to the fact that black people, then referred to as "negroes," were in some obscure way different from us.

I knew nothing of the kind, but I was shocked into an awareness that something was wrong about this arrangement. Such was the prevailing attitude in the Deep South, but I never bought it. It was, in fact, this very boy, Henry, who was responsible for the early development of my social conscience, although it would be a long time before I knew the meaning of those words, and a long time before that social conscience would come to its full fruition.

It was with Henry that I smoked my first cigarette and it was Henry who was sneaked upstairs by my brother and me to spy on our aunt who lived then with my parents and who we managed to glimpse one day as she emerged half-dressed, from her bathroom. It was Henry also, who played with us in the afternoons and who smacked a tennis ball hard up against the side of the house as we all three loved doing. That must have relieved a lot of feelings just as hitting hard on a pillow with a betaka or other object, releases a lot of hostility now.

CHAPTER THREE

Grandmothers, Grandfathers, and Uncle Harry

ice cream and school
lessons and track meets
clearing the hurdles

I HAVE ALREADY WRITTEN ABOUT my difficulties in trying to get my five-year-old hands around the hard black rubber bulb which was the horn on my grandfather's Mercedes. It was a difficulty I never did resolve, as by the time I was old enough and strong enough, we were living in the city and I had other problems. I can imagine that when the horn did sound, people and animals reacted similarly, with fright, perhaps even with terror, but I find it hard at times to be sure that an event in my early memory really happened . . . was it real, or was it only that the story had been told me so often that I believed it to be true?

I have no way of knowing. I recall one trip where we three children were jammed into the front seat with the chauffeur, the youngest cousin not with us, dust flying behind us, chickens squawking in front of us, a horse or two shying away from this monstrous red object, and we proceeding implacably on our triumphant way. Marvelous way to travel. We were the bosses and we knew it!

I was told that this was the first Mercedes in Louisiana, and I imagine that it was. Our family seemed to be first with a lot of things, including later on, cars, planes, speedboats, and such brought in by my uncle Harry. He was the youngest of the four brothers of whom my father was the second oldest. In a strange and almost mystical way, I believe that he, Harry Williams, is responsible for my writing this book. A strong bond always existed between us, and it was on a day a long time ago, while I was pondering this bond, that I felt an urge to write about my youngest uncle.

Harry can best be described as dashing. He was small and slight, and had what I call a gambler's face.

One of my husband's brothers, Carl Tremaine, had a similar look to him, although I don't know exactly what I mean by this. A hardness, a maleness, a devil-may-careness . . . and a sweetness at the same time. Definitely an attractiveness, a come hither look that brought women to his side, certainly in Harry's case, and I would guess in Carl Tremaine's as well.

It is said that Harry was enjoying at one time a torrid affair with a celebrated actress who was on tour with her play. He was himself divorced, but the actress was not, nevertheless the curtain was not allowed to go up until her nightly phone call had come in. He might have been in Timbuctoo and she in San Francisco, it made no difference, she had to hear his voice.

His first wife had been a charming young New York who had left her New York and Southampton life to share Harry's in the wilds of Louisiana. I worshipped Marian with a seven-year old's freely bestowed love until the Sunday when I had come from Sunday school directly to my grandparents' house for a family Sunday dinner. I had brought with me a bright red balloon and was playing with it in the living room when my aunt-by-marriage came down the broad staircase. She looked, as always, lovely, a slender, graceful figure beautifully dressed and, as she descended the stairs, she called to me to toss my balloon her way. Obediently I did what she asked, thrilled no doubt by her attention, but to my horror, as she caught the bright bubble it popped with a loud bang. Her long, tapered fingernails had pierced the thin skin of my balloon and that was the end of that love affair. My balloon meant more to me than aunt Marian's attention. As for her marriage to Uncle Harry, I never knew how that ended.

Harry's next wife was Marguerite Clark, a film star then at the peak of her very successful career, and an adorable, tiny, perfectly formed woman. It was Marguerite who was Disney's model for his animated Snow White, and those of my readers old enough will remember her as playing the part on Broadway as well. It can be imagined that if I had worshipped at the shrine of the charming first wife, I was beside myself with excitement about having a real movie star in the family. Harry preferred living in the country to being in town, so, dutifully, Marguerite permitted herself to be banished to Patterson and to living with his parents when in the city.

Marguerite was an interesting addition to our family. Back in that time, the leading, most popular film star, i.e. biggest box office hit, was Mary Pickford, and right behind her was Marguerite Clark. Marguerite had not married before, although Harry had. She lived with and was ruled by an older sister, who was her agent, her business manager, and everything else you might think of. Curiously, Harry proved to be almost as severe a guardian as her sister had been. He simply buried his wife in the country, and censored her movie contracts so closely that soon she was unable to make any films at all. No bathing suits, no riding clothes, no pants of any kind, no low cut dresses, etc., but Marguerite was so in love with him that she accepted his actions uncomplainingly—at least as far as I knew. And of course Harry was free to live his life how and where he chose.

Harry's passion—at least one of them—was speed. He had the fastest boats on the Atchafalaya river, and my grandparents' garage at their townhouse was home to several of his cars. He had two Isotta Fraschinis, costly, hand-made Italian cars, one for his diminutive wife where the chauffeur's seat was outside of the tonneau while the passenger sat in splendid isolation inside. The other Isotta was a racing model . . . what else? There was still another racing car which had been built for him by his friend, Eddie Rickenbacker. That was clearly his favorite and, when I think of him, it is in that low, dark grey, road burner. There were one or two others I don't recall at the moment. But everything was for speed, which suited both his nature and his appearance.

There was a strong rapport between us which manifested on occasion in unusual ways. Once when I was just about to leave with my husband and his parents on a business trip to California, I had stopped by to say goodbye to my grandmother lying on her pale blue velvet chaise lounge. Harry came into the room to talk with his mother and after, greeting me, he reached into a pocket and drew out a roll of bills. "Here, Honey," he said, "I had a good night last night," and with that he peeled off three hundred dollar bills and handed them to me. "I want you to buy yourself a present from me when you get to California." As he and Ted, my husband, disliked each other intensely, this presented me with a problem. Not to accept the gift, or to accept but not share the fact of it with Ted . . . what to do? What I did was to take it and probably not mention it to Ted, although I don't actually remember. I do remember very well the dress I bought in San Francisco, however . . . a pale rose colored tulle, very delicate, very chic and very feminine. It brings back another lifetime, surely, as I sit here this Sunday morning working, wearing jeans and T-shirt. It almost feels as if I am writing about another woman. And in a very real way, of course, I am.

When I returned from the trip a few weeks later, there was another problem gift. I had been driving a Pierce Arrow roadster, a very fancy car for those days, given me by my parents for my debutante year. It had been a lemon though, often in the shop for one reason or another, and I had left it in New Orleans to have a new paint job while I was away as I had never liked the original green.

My parents' car had met us when we arrived that morning at the station, and after we had dropped Ted off at his office, and before taking me to my own apartment, the chauffeur took me to my parents' house to pick up my car. There sat a freshly painted car, or so I thought, but it actually was more than that. It was a new car that had been bought for me by this same uncle, again a sports model, as I shared his love for sports cars, and still do at eighty-three. This represented a secret gift. I wasn't to tell my husband, who would be furious, the implication of the gift being that if he couldn't afford it himself, at least my uncle could. My mother also came in for Harry's anger, he having told her I was not to know the donor. I drove this car for years. But it put a dot over the eye of our relationship in a curious way. His own wife was certainly not to know, Harry insisted, nor my husband, even me, all of which proved to be impossible, and all of which produced problems. After some male fuming and fussing, Ted had no choice but to accept my acceptance of Harry's gift.

***

Harry had some time earlier formed a partnership with a man who was not only a renowned racing pilot, but who also designed and built racing planes. Jimmy Wedell was his name, and he was, of course, the ideal partner for my uncle. Jimmy held many world speed records in planes of his design, and to this day one of their models—with which Wedell-Williams won many speed trials—hangs in the Smithsonian Museum in Washington, D.C.

Harry founded a small feeder airline, with the hope and intention of seeing it converted into a mail carrier at some future time, but neither he nor Jimmy would live to see it happen. It proved very useful to me once when I was en route to New Orleans from Phoenix and missed my connection in El Paso. The pilot of the commercial plane I was in, which was running late, radioed ahead asking if the Wedell-Williams plane due to depart first for Baton Rouge, then on to New Orleans, would postpone their departure until we arrived and take me on to New Orleans.

Harry was killed in one of his own planes. It was on a night of intense storm activity and he had just left Baton Rouge, where he had spent the day on business. Immediately after takeoff his plane had lost power and crashed into the ground and he was, of course, killed instantly. I was in Arizona by then, with Warren on the Tremaine ranch in the northern part of the state, and I have no trouble remembering the shock and grief that swept over me on hearing of my uncle's death.

Jimmy Wedell, winner of many international speed trophies, was killed not long after when he was giving a flying lesson to a student. The student froze at the controls and went down, taking Jimmy with him.

There is a small museum in Patterson complete with photographs and news clippings about the two men, their lives and numerous accomplishments and of the tragic manner in which their partnership came to its end.

***

My grandfather, F.B. Williams, was a tall slender man. In his last years his pale blue eyes seemed always to be slightly bemused, as if he was finding life more bewildering than he had expected. I would meet him occasionally walking along Canal Street on his way from his office to lunch at his club. My cheery greeting from granddaughter to grandfather would be met with a courteous hand to the brim of his hat and a polite smile. He was uncertain of who exactly I was, it seemed, and I would walk on past without pushing the greeting.

It was not until the final weeks of his life, when he lay in bed, immobilized from a stroke, that I saw him without his toupee. Until that time I had not known that he wore one. On expressing my surprise to my mother, she replied that I was surely the only person in New Orleans who had not observed it, as it inclined always towards being slightly askew.

"F.B.," as everyone called him, was a highly successful business man. He had made a fortune in lumber, and when his cypress holdings were finally gone, no more trees to cut and his several mills closed down and abandoned, he moved from Patterson in to New Orleans, bought a large stone mansion on a man-made hill on prestigious St. Charles Avenue, and addressed himself to investing his fortune and to making his name known in New Orleans. He was a ladies' man, and, I imagine, a considerable womanizer. But he was also a man with a social conscience. He served on various civic boards, gave lavishly of his money to projects for those less fortunate, and soon had become a man of importance in the civic, financial, and social life of New Orleans.

Pere loved entertaining and did so on a grand scale and consequently his house became a center where hospitality was legendary. My grandmother, Mere, knew how to entertain, and although she herself lived most of her life on the second floor, being a semi-invalid, the household was under her firm control and they knew it. In spite of her soft look, and equally soft voice, she was a woman of iron will. She was a real politician's wife, and although I knew that Pere had turned down the opportunity to run for governor of the state, I was aware that he represented power not only in Louisiana but nationally as well. F.B. wielded great influence in many areas of his life and the life of the city he had chosen to live in. I remember on one night when I was at the theater in New York with my grandfather, a man came out on the stage to introduce him to the audience. He referred to him as F.B. Willliams, "the lumber baron of Louisiana," and Pere was asked to stand and take a bow. I believe we were seeing the Ziegfield Follies, and I was ecstatic with pride.

Pere's idea of inviting friends to a football game, was to charter a private car, on whatever line went into that particular city where either Tulane University or Louisiana State University was playing, and inviting a generous handful of friends to accompany him. Being his granddaughter, I was not among the privileged, but I can imagine that those trips were highlights in numerous lives.

My grandparents' house itself, a large, ugly, yet impressive structure, was reached either by walking up three flights of shallow, stone steps leading from the sidewalk to the front door, or by driving grandly up a rising, curving driveway and being deposited at the covered porte cochere at the side of the house. If you came in the front door, you rang the bell and the butler would welcome you into the large open area at the bottom of the stairway.

Writing the above has just given me a possible insight into my grandparents. Suddenly I am picturing my grandfather, a tall, attractive young man, motivated by who knows what family situations, perhaps a mother who was scornful of his achievements, maybe an unattainable girlfriend who challenged him to "do as well as so-and-so does," or perhaps only a young post-Civil War Southerner determined to "show those Yankees what we can do." Possibly he was urged on by an ambitious young bride. Who knows, but something certainly pushed him into indulging a pretentious life style.

Beyond and slightly below the main house, stood a separate stone building that housed a large and fascinating collection of cars. There were sleeping quarters for the servants above. In addition to Harry's cars, Pere had a Rolls Royce that went with my grandparents on their alternate yearly trips to Europe as well as to Atlantic City. I, like my grandfather, adored the boardwalk paralleling the white beach below, the rumbling sounds caused by the rolling chairs, the saltwater taffy stands or the trinket shops, as well as Atlantic City's incredible Elephant Hotel which stood somewhat outside of the city itself and was, really and truly, a building constructed in the shape of an elephant.

While Pere had his Rolls Royce, my grandmother was always driven in a large limousine called a White. It was dark blue in color and awkward in design. I never saw another or heard of anyone else having a White. I seem to remember that the White company manufactured trucks, tour buses, etc. A small blue Buick was also a part of the collection, and this was for Peter, my grandmother's chauffeur, to use when marketing, doing errands, and so forth.

Back in those days, your car went along with you on whatever was the liner of your choice, and often as not the owner would then drive, or be driven, to Paris or London, depending on his destination, thereby eliminating frustrating delays along the way. In my grandparents' case, they always took Peter Pellegrini, my grandmother's Italian chauffeur, to Europe with them. He was fluent in several languages, and they would sail through Europe in the big, black Rolls with the Louisiana plates which described the limitless joys of hunting and fishing in that far off place.

Pere was a frightening figure to me, my contacts with him being so minimal. My remembrances circulate around sarcastic remarks about my clothes, my hair, and other such charming liberties grownups so often take with young members of their families. I now realize they were actually aimed at the in-law (my mother's) side of the family and that my dress, hair, behavior, etc. were of no consequence whatever, simply the peg to hang the hat on.

***

My paternal grandmother, Mere, would have made an excellent wife for a man in any government. She was a truly political woman, subscribed to every important newspaper in the country, read them all, and absorbed and digested them as well. I have a vivid picture of her lying on her pale blue velvet chaise lounge, dressed in a delicate garment of chiffon and lace from one of the great fashion houses of Paris. Her silver hair was piled on top of her head, and as the chaise lounge was backed by windows, the light streaming in often caused a nebulous halo to appear to surround her. Newspapers were scattered everywhere on the floor by her side, and if the day were a bit chilly, there would be a chinchilla robe over her feet.

She loved to whistle, and sometimes could be heard walking quietly about her domain, whistling a tuneless little song softly under her breath. Her domain was the spacious second story of the house. There were, as I recall, half a dozen or more bedrooms and probably at least that many baths besides two or three smaller rooms, work rooms for pressing, sewing or such. All of the rooms opened onto a large common room, just as downstairs, and the broad staircase ascending from below ended in that room. Sofas and chairs were there, besides tables and another chaise for Mere to stretch out on when she tired of her bedroom.

Very little escaped her notice. She spoke with an acid tongue when she felt so inclined, and she disliked my mother intensely as she did at least two of her other daughters-in-law. I suspect her dislike for my mother involved her own feelings about her son, my father. Whatever the reason, her feelings involved my own, naturally, as I would be divided between loyalty to my mother, outrage that she was so misunderstood by her mother-in-law, and the natural wish to please my grandmother. Perhaps she was goading me. I wouldn't have put it past her, a test of sorts, but which side was I supposed to be on?

Mere was an experienced and gracious hostess. Recalling some of the guest lists, I cannot doubt that often they included Pere's current crush, complete with husband to balance the table . . . or someone's conscience perhaps. At times those dinners were interesting. It was there that I met Huey Long, embarking on his first campaign and seeking backing from my grandfather. It was a dinner of paradoxes. Power was meeting power and all sorts of events were set in motion that night that were totally unknown to me. The red-faced spellbinder from upstate Louisiana sat at the lace covered table of one of the state's most important men, in a house that every politician in Louisiana would have given his eye teeth to be invited to. The meal progressed from oyster gumbo, through fish, through main course, to salad and finally dessert. Long's joviality never flagged, nor did Pere's watchful manner, and I always regretted not being quite old enough to have had any real interest in politics or politicians.

Mere's blue eyes were set in a face that I still think of as a pussycat face. She wore a habitual expression of amused secrecy, as if she knew something the rest of us didn't know and which she wasn't about to tell. She had two close women friends, one a gentle soul, the wife of her doctor, the other a tough-minded town gossip. Mere was a woman of extreme intelligence, although I do not put her in the category of an intellectual. The practical matters of the government and the military were her burning concerns. Art, philosophy and the humanities held no interest for her. She was a mine of information on subjects pertaining to politics, economics, and world affairs, though she never went to a concert, never went to the opera or a play. Pere, on the other hand, had front row seats for every popular musical in New York whenever they visited that city.

***

Grandmother, my mother's mother, was most definitely an intellectual, as were the other members of her Jewish family. She scandalized them by marrying a non-Jew, my maternal grandfather whom I never knew, and I rather think that some of them never forgave her. Her family loved music, played various instruments, and in general supported the arts as well as civic affairs. They sent their sons to Europe on Grand Tours in the old-fashioned way feeling that they must be exposed to other cultures, they dressed their wives and daughters in clothes from Paris, and altogether graced the world by their gentle charm and kindness.

Lyons Page, one of the men in that family was mentally retarded, and it was always hard for me to be in his presence. It was my own hangup making me fearful, however, as he was a loving soul with two burning passions, in his life, music was one and perfumes the other. His record collection was impressive, as was his knowledge of the classics. Every available inch of space in his room, or the sitting room he shared with his mother, was covered with exotic bottles of perfume. He was short and somewhat overweight and spoke with a husky voice. His eager welcomes frightened me a bit, and I suffered for his mother who appeared to me doomed forever to be chained to her son. There was another son, married with children of his own, and when I wondered what would happen to the retarded one, I supposed it would be the obligation of the older brother to care for the younger sibling. But with the knowledge that I have gained over the years, I realize that living with this gentle soul may have been a very enriching experience.

I recently witnessed a touching demonstration of love from a young Downs' syndrome man. He was visiting his aunt, who lived at the time in my guest house. She and I were standing in my kitchen talking one afternoon when he came into the house. He walked over to his aunt, stood close to her, and put his arm over her shoulder. I smiled at him and teasingly asked him if he liked her. He answered that he did, then I said, "And do you love her?" He tightened his arm around her and said, "All the time."

The house my Jewish family lived in was dark and very depressing to me. In fact, many of those Victorian New Orleans houses affected me in this way. The tall windows were invariably hung with heavy dark curtains, often velvet or brocade, and always totally shutting out the sun. As my idea of a house is to invite the sun inside, to have light spilling from as many sources as possible, it follows that I couldn't be in sympathy with heavily carved mahogany and knickknacks everywhere, in short a room full of darkness and dustcatchers.

The house next door to this one however, was quite different. Aunt Eva, whom I haven't yet mentioned, was the matriarch of this Jewish family, grandmother to the retarded man, mother to his mother, and one of her sons lived in the house next door. Uncle George was this cousin's name, and to me he and his wife were Cousin George and Cousin Anna.

I liked Cousin Anna and enjoyed going to their house, not quite so dark as the one next door. I have retained a picture of her all of my life. She had been ill and was still recuperating when I entered her room on that sunny morning. She lay in her huge mahogany four-poster bed piled high with lace and embroidered pillows. Cousin Anna reclined against them, her lower body covered with a linen sheet, and her upper body by a robe of fine white muslin. Her masses of shining white hair were piled on top of her head. The morning sun was streaming into the room through the slatted window blinds and creating patterns on the dark floor. It was a hot summer morning in New Orleans. Two or three small grass rugs lay scattered about on the highly polished floors. A little breeze touched white muslin curtains, just enough to move them slightly and further the effect of peaceful harmony in this room. That picture has never left me. In a way it epitomizes for me a certain way of life, a certain pleasant way in a southern city on a hot summer morning.

***

The house I grew up after we had moved into town was in a small private park in New Orleans. A gravel driveway ran past three houses before circling around an eliptical planted area to pass three more opposite the first three.

Ours was the middle house on the first side, with a childless couple on our left, and a fairly elderly couple on the right. This couple had one son, a boy close in age to my brother and myself, and we sometimes made fun of him because he invariably answered his mother's frequent calls with a never-failing courteous: "Yes, Mother." We had nothing against politeness, but somehow this seemed to us as going a bit far.

With a close friend I spent many afternoons high in the branches of a camphor tree playing our ongoing game of inventing new personas for ourselves. There was a little trouble once, I recall, over the question of a name. One of us had chosen the name of Patria, the other, Jane, and when we wanted to combine the two for a special project, there might be a difference of opinion as to which name should precede the other. There must have been a definite squabble for me to recall it after so long a time, but those after-school hours in the fragrant leafy camphor trees were a major part of my growing up years and I can enjoy them in retrospect.

Our house was what I think of as typically southern. It was white with massive columns across the broad front porch. Rising from the spacious entrance was a wide staircase. The stairs rose gracefully to pause on a landing where there was a small room, furnished with a desk and one or two chairs. Then the stairs turned back towards the front of the house, and the effect was to give even more space to the rooms. The staircase was free standing, thus open beneath the topmost part. Underneath, the telephone sat on a small table with a chair beside it.

Louise Jonas Nixon, our maternal grandmother, was herself a prominent figure in the civic and social life of New Orleans. It was she who was the principal founder of the Little Theatre in New Orleans, the first in the country, I believe, and she acted also in many of the plays presented there. True to the French heritage in New Orleans, the theatre was called by its French name, and became famous as Le Petit Theatre du Vieux Carre, the Little Theatre of the Old Quarter. This charming theatre is in an old building close by Jackson Square in the very heart of the French Quarter.

At one time Grandmother was given a decoration by the French government for her part in spearheading the movement to restore the French Quarter which had become virtually a slum. There are many buildings of historic significance in the Quarter, many with wrought iron fences and balustrades of a quality not found any more. Bringing this historically significant area back to life was a major undertaking. Excellent smaller hotels stand throughout the Quarter, bed and breakfast places along with glittering tourist hotels, complete with lobbies hung with crystal chandeliers, specialty restaurants, bars, night clubs, and convention halls. There are tiny shops selling trinkets, and praline kitchens presided over by the traditionally racist depiction of a black woman, hands folded over ample stomach, presumably the maker of the candies sold inside. There are restaurants by the dozens, famous ones, pretentious ones, family ones, and it is hard to find one that couldn't serve you something you would like.

The city is renowned for its food, and rightly so. It is also a gold mine for searchers of antiques, and all day, everyday, tourists can be seen walking up and down Royal Street, peering in dusty windows and haggling with shop keepers. When I lived there, I recall one dealer who had an interesting way of providing the antiques, although he did not pretend that they were. I was looking for a dining room table, and found that the ones I wanted were all too expensive. He suggested that he make me one, but I protested that the patina would be lacking and that it would clearly be a new table. "Not so," he assured me, and showed me what he often did. When an old piece was in too much disrepair for restoration, he carefully disassembled it, laying the wood aside until he had a use for it. He then showed me the wood he had in mind, and I was convinced. The wood was beautiful, as was the table when it was built, and the price was far less than the antique had been.

CHAPTER FOUR

A Sky Full Of Balloons

school
balloons
and growing up

THE YEAR I WAS TWELVE was a memorable one for me. For one thing I was permitted for the first time in my life to go to school alone on the New Orleans streetcar. Before this I had been driven by the family chauffeur, and whereas this might seem to some readers as nothing to complain about, my burning desire was to be like every-one else, and although a few of my friends were driven in their family's cars too, it wasn't free enough for me. I wanted to be my own person, and being on the street car alone gave me the sense of glorious independence I needed.

On the short walk from the small park-like area where we lived to St. Charles Avenue where the street-car ran, I would be accompanied by my governess, and this walk was definitely enlivened by the fact that the boy I was currently in love with lived in one of the houses we passed on our way to the corner. At age twelve I was so besotted by this boy that in the late afternoons I sometimes sat in the window in my room hoping against hope to see my loved one walking past on his way home from football practice. When I did, my little heart would do flip-flops and I would sometimes call his name, timidly, to be sure, but at least I had made contact.

For some obscure reason I had a favorite streetcar, number 421, and as I took the streetcar at approximately the same time each morning, I often had the experience of being on 421. Believe it or not, about 1987, the last time I was in New Orleans, I saw that very same streetcar racketing down St. Charles Avenue just as in the past. At the time I rode it to school, 421 was one of the brand-new fleet just put into service in New Orleans. It was light green and seemed long, low, and rakish compared to the older ones just retired. Even the flat clang of the bell activated by the operator, the signal that we were about to move, was exciting to me.

I remember one day when I sat close by the open window, resting my arm on the sill, holding my chin on my hand. I was making wild faces and thrusting my tongue here and there in my mouth, impersonating a young lady suffering from a toothache, a ruse intended to gain both the attention and the sympathy of my fellow passengers, including of course, the attractive man sitting just behind me. I had already discovered that illness was a good way to get my mother's attention, and I hadn't yet absorbed the advice of one of her favorite maxims. "You wouldn't worry so much about what others think of you if you realized how seldom they do." I have often quoted that to others but I'm not at all sure that I have ever taken it totally to heart myself. I appreciate its truth, still, at times when self-consciousness surfaces, I smile and stand a little straighter.

On another day I happened to glance over the shoulder of the passenger in the seat just ahead and read the shocking news of the demise of the famous old French Opera House. It had burned to the ground during the night and had been declared a total loss. This Opera House had been the first to be built in the entire country, and a great many world-famous singers had given their initial North American performances there. It had played an enormously important part in the cultural life of the city, and there was no doubt that its loss was a major one. I had been accustomed all my life to hearing my mother singing or humming arias from various operas, which added greatly to my own appreciation when I was older and had that lifelong familiarity to add to my enjoyment.

But that morning, aside from my sense of shock and sorrow, was the exciting realization that for once I had learned something of real interest to my whole family, and that I was probably the first one to have heard it. In a way the streetcar was a connection for me with the outside world. I was in touch with strangers and was free to give whatever meaning to them and to their actions as I could.

Maybe even more exciting than riding the streetcar alone was being able to choose my lunch at school. I was proving that nutrition is very much a matter of selection.

This involved a certain amount of deception, lying is a more accurate word, and meant that I was skirting dangerously close to real trouble when I told my mother in the evenings what I had had for lunch, which in no way came close to what I had actually bought and eaten with relish.

The rattling streetcar deposited me on a corner about two blocks from school. Almost always there was time for me to run into the drugstore on the corner and get a five-cent bag of peanut candies. For those who have never seen these delicacies, they are shaped exactly like a real peanut shell except for having a shiny look to them. The shells are crunchy and the insides soft, as in peanut butter. Armed with this hedge against starvation, I would march into my classroom and carefully insert my treasure in my desk, concealing it under the cover of the lid. From there on it was all gravy, you might say.

When lunchtime came around I would go with everyone else and inspect the blackboard where the menus were displayed. I would select a wholly fictitious choice, beefstew, tuna salad, etc, whatever I thought might please my mother who was probably ordering something marvelous at Galatoire's or Antoine's just about then. But what I bought was always the same as I had bought the day before and would on the day following: chocolate ice cream, a small bag of potato chips, and a sour pickle. These, coupled with my peanut candy, comprised my lunch every single day of that school year. Sweet, sour, and salt. Delicious!

Twenty-odd years ago I had a hysterectomy, and on the following morning when I was barely awake there came a soft knock on the door. Around the half-opened door of my room appeared the head of a friend wearing a large cowboy hat. The owner of the head was carrying a cake that he had baked for me the previous day. As it was Halloween he had trimmed his cake with peanut candies and those small yellow and white sugar candies that are supposed to look like grains of corn. He was aware of my fondness for cheap candy, and I have seldom been as touched as on that morning when Paul brought me that cake. You have to love a friend who would do that. And seeing those yellow and white candies, I almost felt twelve years old again.

Another landmark of being twelve was having my first period. I must have been singularly naive and totally uninformed, as I was shocked and horrified. My mother had never talked about it to me, and evidently none of my friends had either. I recalled this years later when I was giving Katy, my younger daughter, similar information. Her sister, Diana, had just begun her period. Realizing that I would have to tell Katy some of the facts of life, so to speak, I did the best I could. Katy looked at me in horror and said firmly, "Well, all I can say is, that's never going to happen to me."

My mother told me of having often locked me in a closet as a means of punishment for some sin, and to my shame I once employed the same tactic with my son, then a small child, an event on which I would rather not dwell. My mother, however, considered it a suitable punishment for a child and told of one day when I had been in the closet for quite some time. She and my nurse had approached the closet, asking if I was ready to come out, to which I answered no, that I liked it in there.

Obviously, this wasn't true, but I was not about to admit defeat.

There was a time when it was hard for me to receive from others. It stemmed, I believe, from wanting to be independent, not wanting to have to depend on my mother. If my older brother was so marvelous, my thinking must have gone, then I could be independent, too. Part of this thinking became a reluctance to accept from others. Happily I long ago conquered this feeling. Now I sometimes warn people not to offer help unless they mean it, as I am liable to accept. Like all of us, I too need help at times. I too am vulnerable, insecure, all of those things and more, and I also am aware of how valuable others can be. So I say, "Yes, thank you," to my helper, then another little thank you to God for providing that helper.

***

When I was not quite fourteen I was sent away to boarding school. My lungs have always been my most vulnerable part, and it was decided that what I needed was high country. So off I went to Lake Placid in the Adirondacks. The Montemare School was newly formed. Our spring and fall terms were spent in the mountains of New York state, while the winter term saw us in Miami Beach.

Lots of new experiences came my way at that time. I was unfamiliar with snow and ice, and although I never became very proficient at either ice skating or skiing, I had a lot of fun trying. I recall the first day I arrived my mother talked with one of the older students, a girl of nineteen doing graduate work, and my mother addressed her as Miss whatever her name was. I was appalled and awed, and asked my mother if I would have to do that too. When she assured me that as a fellow student I could use her first name, you can't imagine my relief.

Boarding school was a tremendous learning experience. I learned about living communally, about sports that I had never tried, quite a bit about human nature (in spite of my youth), and, luckily for me, about how not to become addicted to drugs. At that time there was a popular cleaning fluid called Carbona. It was what I used when I needed to clean my clothes. One freezing cold night, when I had closed the one window in my tiny box-like room and was working away on a spot on my uniform, I became aware that the strong fumes were giving me a very pleasant feeling. I was slightly dizzy, slightly euphoric, and quite on the verge of being overcome. I enjoyed it so much that I continued this for a few nights, until finally one of the teachers came into my room, smelled the cleaning fluid, and asked me in startled tones what on earth was happening. Being completely naive, I explained the process by which I had arrived at this state of being, whereupon she gave me such a lecture that I was terrified, and I never again experimented with cleaning fluid or anything else.

There were two boys' schools on the same schedule as ours, so we did on occasion get to have a bit of socializing. I remember magic sleigh rides through snowy woods at night with lanterns hung on the horses' harnesses lighting the way. I remember that I was a bit of a basketball star as well as the organist for the morning and evening hymns, and how important I felt when I sprained my finger playing basketball with the resultant swelling preventing me from playing the organ, which I disliked anyway. I further recall having to have a plain gold ring cut from my swollen finger, which was very distressing for me.

I spent three years at the Montemare School, and went on to what was then called Miss Bennett's. At that time it was a two-year finishing school and has long since become a two-year junior college that my daughter Diana attended later on. This school was situated in New York on the Hudson River on beautiful rolling grounds.

What did I learn at Miss Bennett's? I learned to play basketball, to ice skate, to play hockey, to ski, to ride sidesaddle, and to jump my horse in horse shows. I learned how to get along with people, and I learned how to avoid one lesbian woman. And I also learned a bit about boys. All in all, my teenage years gave me much valuable material to live by for the rest of my life.

I even learned some academic things as well. I had a history teacher whom I really disliked, but when it came around to the Civil War, well, she was from Tennessee and I from Louisiana, so at last we had a meeting of Southern minds. My favorite subjects were literature and creative writing. I ignored mathematics as much as possible.

***

Although many years have passed since my teenage days, one particular event remains indelibly etched on the screen of my mind:

On this day I was attending some sort of fair or bazaar. I was with the current suitor of the moment. This boy and I had a long and occasionally ardent relationship for some years. He was The Important Person in my life for quite some time, but this day brings only recollections of balloons. They were being sold at the fair, and Jack asked me if I would like a balloon. I looked at that many colored cluster of shimmering bubbles all straining upwards under the hot tropical sun and somewhat to my own surprise replied that I wanted them all. They seemed to me to be trying to break free from the confining strings attached to each one.

My obliging companion presented me with the cluster. As soon as I had it in my hand, I opened my fingers and let them all go. We stood transfixed, as did a lot of others, and watched them soar up, up into the blueness above until finally they were lost to sight. And then I threw my arms around Jack and kissed him, thanking him for having given me such a beautiful gift.

I have often reflected on that event and am convinced it held enormous importance for me. I believe it may have been the first conscious act of defiance against my mother. I have all of my life been passionately addicted to the idea of being my own person, and having been brought up in a proper manner I thought this wasn't easy to achieve. In letting the balloons go free, it was really myself soaring to the sky. So Jack, if you should ever read this book, thank you for helping me on my way.

CHAPTER FIVE

Here's To The Queen

the glittering debutante
how little I knew

TIME FASCINATES ME. Clearly we invented the concept a long time ago, but to date no one I have asked knows exactly where and when it was first considered. It surely was thought up by an agricultural people who, observing the effects of dark and light, sun and moon, hot and cold, upon the crops and upon themselves, felt it expedient to divide these puzzling facts into some sort of order.

There is a distinct possibility that these experiments were first made in the Valley of the Euphrates, in the lush area known as the Fertile Crescent. We are the inheritors of their experience, although sometimes I think to call us the victims might be more appropriate.

Time rules us inexorably. We are in truth its slaves, and it may just be the strongest of all the self-imposed bonds we wind around ourselves. "I have another appointment in fifteen minutes. . . ." or, "I want to stay but I have to be. . . ." etc., etc.

Two friends in the past three days have given me the identical analogy for someone writing an autobiography. I picture myself rowing a boat. Ahead of me, or should I say behind me, is the future. Although I face backwards, I am steadily moving forward into whatever lies ahead. I must look behind me often to avoid the unseen pitfalls of my voyage, my future.

My attention and my physical effort are occupied with what is in front of the boat, but as I look in front of me, I am observing what has already happened, the route I have just traveled. So in deciding to write about my life, I must maintain my goal of constant forward motion while simultaneously reviewing the past. To further complicate this already paradoxical situation, as all this is happening I sit firmly grounded in the present moment in that elusive concept we call Time.

***

New Orleans is renowned for its annual festival, Mardi Gras. When the formal invitation arrived to request my presence as Rex's Queen on the following twenty-sixth day of February in the year nineteen-hundred-and-twenty-six, it did not come as a total surprise for me. Rex was always chosen from the ranks of prominent New Orleans' businessmen, and I was a debutante that year. There had been rumors for some time that I was to be honored as Queen.

I was excited and happy, and needless to say, wanted immediately to sit down with my mother and talk it over. There would be a myriad of details that would be our responsibility to decide, though the theme of the ball had of course long since been agreed upon by the ruling committees.

I understand that plans for the next year's ball are under way immediately after the curtain has fallen on the elaborately decorated stage where the current one has just been held, so that by the time the frock-coated invitation committee arrived at our house precisely at eleven o'clock on a Sunday morning in early autumn, only the acceptances of the Queen and her Court remained to be finalized. Our responses, of course, were taken for granted, as it would have been unheard of for the elegantly dressed gentlemen sitting in our living room to be surprised with a "no" answer. I doubt that this has ever happened, or indeed, ever will happen.

On Mardi Gras Day, I awoke to an electric atmosphere of excitement. The servants in the house were beside themselves, as in New Orleans there are but two important people in the whole city on that day, and I was one of them. The other, of course, was the King, Rex himself. So my glory was reflected in them and I saw only smiling faces on that day.

There was a ritual to the day and we followed it to the letter. The Queen and her court of eight or ten other debutantes all gathered at my house at ten o'clock in the morning to be photographed, before being driven downtown where we were to greet our "subjects." We sat for two hours or more on the balcony of the Boston Club, an old and exclusive men's club, while hundreds of thousands of gaudily costumed people below on the broad expanse of Canal Street milled about to get better positions so they could say that they had seen the Queen and her court.

Skirts were short that year, and my periwinkle blue chiffon dress followed the fashion. It was made with long sleeves and a scoop neck. With it I wore a floppy brim-med hat of soft felt dyed to match the dress. This was before we had been made aware that queens and such publicly viewed people should affect small brimless hats, the better to permit their public to see them. When Grace Kelly became the Princess of Monaco a few years later, we heard the newsmen comment on the fact that her lovely face was almost completely hidden by her floppy brimmed hat.

If you have been in New Orleans on Mardi Gras Day or seen it on TV, you will know the sight that greeted us when we stepped out onto the balcony that morning. We were to view the parade as it passed in front of the Boston Club, which was almost as packed with people inside and on the balcony as were the streets in front of us. They were there by invitation and were families and friends of members, an honor that was vied for by many for some time before The Day.

When the Rex parade appeared the excitement grew intense. It is customary for the people lining the parade routes to shout up to the maskers on the floats. "Throw me a Mardi Gras, mister!" is heard from all sides, and the men on the floats oblige by tossing down the trinkets they have bought for the occasion. As the parade drew close to the balcony where we sat, one of the club's attendants appeared with a ladder that he leaned against the side of the King's float when it had halted in front of our balcony. The club's president, meticulously dressed in morning coat and striped trousers, then climbed up the ladder and presented His Majesty with a glass of sparkling champagne, whereupon Rex arose from his throne, lifted his glass high in a toast to the Queen, drank. then dashed the glass to the ground where it shattered in a thousand pieces. This would insure that no other toast would ever be drunk from that glass. The smashing of the glass was the signal for us to go into the club where a lavish buffet waited, and for all of us, the Queen and her court, to mingle with the invited guests gathered there both to see and to be seen.

I was presented with an enormous and rather appalling bouquet of daffodils, violets, and green leaves. There was a pie-shaped wedge of violets, another of daffodils, with the third of green leaves. Rex's official colors are purple, yellow, and green, so this traditional bouquet is presented to each queen. The resultant massing of colors makes for a stiff and awkward bouquet, and as it was, in my memory, at the very least eighteen inches across, and probably larger, it wasn't exactly easy to handle. But it was fun, gloriously heady fun, and for the several hours we were to sit on that balcony I don't doubt any of us thought of much else than the excitement we were experiencing.

Realizing that the hundreds of thousands of people amassed on the streets below were there to see us, and in particular to see me, I have to confess that, sitting here writing about it after all these years, it seems as if it took place on another planet.

It was a day and night that I had to live with split-second precision. You know that you have to be in the right place at the exact right moment. Our family chauffeur drove me both day and night, and I could sense it was as if he were intensely participating in my own excitement. We, the other girls and myself, were all driven to our respective homes around two o'clock in the afternoon to have a short rest before the night's activities.

We had sat for hours on the balcony, had mingled with the guests at the luncheon table, and had watched the Rex parade when the lead float bearing the King himself stopped in front of the Boston Club.

That night I was again driven to the Boston Club, after first being photographed with the King, our two train-bearing pages, and all the Court, which by now included the Dukes as well as the Maids of Honor. The Dukes were all young businessmen and included Ted Simmons, the man of my dreams whom I planned to marry in a few weeks. The photographing took place at my house, and after a light buffet supper we once more took off for the ceremonies to follow.

This time I was alone in the car with all the interior lights blazing. I had a motorcycle escort, a policeman on either side of the car, and with sirens wailing we sped through the city. And did I feel important!

Once more we emerged onto the balcony. Once more we experienced the heady sensation of being the focus of all eyes. Once more the morning's routine was repeated, and this time it was all glitter and light. Night crowds are noisier than the earlier ones, as by this time plenty of celebrating had been going on. The crowd's enthusiasm only made it more exciting for me.

I inclined my crowned head from side to side in what I hoped was a gracious manner, waved my heavily jeweled scepter a bit nervously, and absolutely loved the whole thing. My gown was a copy of the one worn by Empress Josephine at her coronation, and I glittered from head to foot. Every inch of the heavy white satin was covered with rhinestones and tiny crystal bugles. It was made with a high waist, known as an Empire waist, and ended in its own train, two or three feet long. The traditional train that hung from my shoulders was of gold cloth bordered with ermine. It was six feet long and was so beautifully designed that I actually did not feel its great weight. By then I was so keyed up that it might have been cutting into my flesh and I would have been oblivious.

Our night was a long one. After reviewing the Comus parade, which in itself is a long procedure, we prepared for the final event. We paraded around the ballroom and then joined Comus, his Queen, and his Court on the double throne where we were to reign jointly over the Carnival Ball. The decorations were gorgeous, the costumes breathtaking, and the entire thing a really magnificent spectacle.

The members of the organization who host the ball, all men, are dressed in costumes and wear elaborate masks. They are called the maskers. The maskers, including the one who sent you the invitation, were liable to be fairly well along in celebrating. You generally recognized them, of course, while pretending not to.

Their heads were adorned with shoulder-length wigs, topped by hats in keeping with the theme of the ball. Their hands were covered by heavy gauntleted gloves, and their legs were often encased in knee britches and tights, with their feet in fancy slippers.

If you received a "call out" card enclosed with your ball invitation, you were seated in a special section, all women, there to chat with your friends while waiting to be "called out" to dance with whatever masker was inviting you to dance. The men who formed the call-out committee were dressed formally in white tie and tails, and the procedure was as follows. A masker on the dance floor would tell a member of the call-out committee that he wanted to dance with you. The committee man, if he knew you, would catch your eye and signal you or come to get you. If you were not known to the committee man, he would stand next to the call-out section, calling out your name. Then he would lead you on to the dance floor. Incidentally, after the fifth dance, the committee men were permitted to dance, too, but only they and the maskers, no other men.

***

So much was crowded into my life during that exciting year of being a debutante. To cap it off, on the Sunday following Mardi Gras Day, my parents formally announced my engagement to Ted, with the wedding to take place in April when the Lenten season was over.

Having been brought up in the Episcopal Church, there were some rules, I discovered, not unlike those in the Catholic Church, and one of them was that marriages could not take place during Lent. There was one day when this was excepted, and that was St. Joseph's Day.

The wedding took place on a warm April night in Christ Church Cathedral on St. Charles Avenue. Again I had a police motorcycle escort, since my so recently being Rex's queen had prompted many curious onlookers to collect at the church in order to see me. In fact, when my grandparents arrived regally in their Rolls Royce, policemen had to clear a path for them through the crowd so they could walk from their automobile to the door of the cathedral. From there they proceeded up the aisle to their seats in the front row.

It was, you might say, a big bash. I had ten bridesmaids, Ted was attended by ten groomsmen, the full choir sang, and the dean of the cathedral performed the ceremony. The bridesmaids wore tulle dresses of shades ranging from the palest pink to deep rose. I wore a floor-length creamy-white satin gown with sleeves girdled in small bands of pearls. My head dress was a fitted cap of tulle, held in place by a circlet of pearls, with a long, full tulle veil billowing back over the gown and train. We had a big reception at my parents' house afterwards, and then Ted and I took a late-night train to Pass Christian on the Mississippi Gulf Coast, there to spend our honeymoon.

Kit's father, Laurence Moore Williams, at left of portrait with his three brothers—Harry Palmerston Williams, in sailor suit; Charles Seyburn Williams, eldest of the brothers; and Lewis Kemper Williams. Photo taken in late nineteenth century.

Williams' company store in Patterson, Louisiana, where Kit was born. "I remember this little building as large, dark, cavernous and filled with wonders. My brother, our cousins, Steve and Teddy Seyburn, and I would walk there and buy candy and sodas."

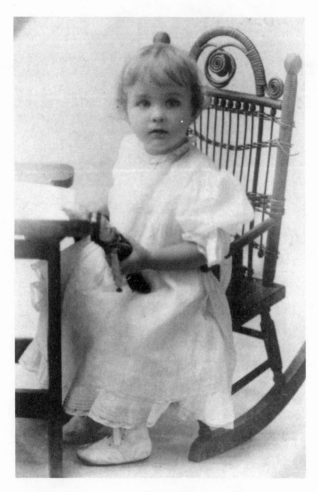

*Kit Williams at two years with doll in rock-
ing chair.*

Kit as a child in France.

Kit with Laurence in Paris.

Kit with mother and Laurence, New Orleans, c. 1912.

Kit, around age 12, in New Orleans.

Kit with her brother, Laurence, and her grandmother, Mere, Mrs. Frank Bennett Williams.

Kit as Queen of Oberon, 1926 (Krewe).

Kit as Rex's Queen, 1926. Rex was Joseph P. Henican, a prominent cotton broker. The page on Kit's right is Homer Dupuy, subsequently a successful doctor and lifelong friend.

CHAPTER SIX

My Visit To The Money Lender and Other Happenings

money is scarce
I borrow to pay bills
a joke on me

I SEE NOW HOW I have tried to please the men in my life, no matter what the issue. On searching for the answer as to why, I confess that it was always because of a fear that I might lose the particular man in question.

I learned to smoke to please a man who was several years older than I and who had actually been a Marine! This was glamour too strong to resist, and I dutifully puffed away on dates with him until I was an "experienced" smoker. This, incidentally, resulted in my becoming a heavy smoker for many years. Finally, on a fishing trip in Ireland some twenty-five years ago, I contracted a severe cold and it was the Irish doctor in the hotel whose warning really affected me. He was listening to my chest, and when he had finished, I lit a cigarette. He was stunned. His words still resound in my head. "With that chest, you're smoking!" he exclaimed.

Whereupon he gave me a little lecture on the subject of my heart and its connection to smoking. He frightened me, and in a few weeks I knew I was going to stop.

But back in the days when I was pinning magnolia blossoms on the underside of the brim of a large floppy straw hat . . . leghorn straw it was, with a black velvet ribbon around the crown . . . back then my thoughts were far from psychological, let alone philosophical or metaphysical. In that time, both as the pampered daughter of wealthy parents, then as the wife of a promising young businessman, I thought more of the exciting life I led. What could be more important than bridge tournaments, horseback riding along the levees, playing my Steinway baby grand, a wedding gift from Ted's parents, or nine holes of golf with my husband, himself a golfer of championship quality?

From this era and this particular pursuit comes the remembrance of a motto of Ted's. When I would miss a putt by a short margin, a common occurrence, Ted would say to me, "Shoot boldly for the hole, babe. Better to overshoot than to stop on the rim of the cup." I have found this to be useful advice in almost all situations. In other words, whatever the project, at least give it a good try.

Ted Simmons was a charming man, tall, good-looking, brown eyes and hair, and a loose-limbed way of handling his body and walk. So charming, in fact, that before we married he was looked upon with covetous eyes by practically every sub-deb, debutante, and on into the older post-debutante group in New Orleans. When he was a groomsman in a big wedding, he almost seemed

to "give the party" as he stood at the entrance to the
church, smiling and offering his immaculately tailored
arm to some lady fortunate enough to be escorted down
the aisle by him. My grandmother remarked to me once
that I was making a mistake in marrying him, as "No
woman should marry a professional charmer."

But I did. I was so strongly attracted to Ted, that
although I would from time to time find other men
alluring and sometimes would think that now I had
gotten over my passion for Ted, it never failed that when
I saw him or even heard his voice on the telephone, I
was instantly once again his slave.

Our idyll lasted for only a year or two before I
realized that the paths we were choosing, my husband
and I, were already leading in vastly different directions.

In addition to being an alcoholic, Ted was a com-
pulsive gambler. His salary was not large and we tried to
live on it, but the added burden of his gambling often
pushed us over the edge. When I sat each month at my
desk wrestling with bills, some of which spanned periods
of several months, paying one a few dollars to show that
I was aware of the debt, others perhaps going straight
into the wastebasket before even being opened, I was
assured by my profligate husband that in order to maintain credit this was the way it had to be done.

"Never pay your bills in full. If you do that you will
lose your credit rating," was his advice to me. When I
would ask him how much he thought his gambling cost
us, he told me that the law of averages never failed,
therefore it stood to reason that his losses and gains
balanced each other. I wonder why I was the one to deal

with the paperwork. Perhaps because I had always seen my mother doing it.

So one day, faced with the mounting bills, I took my courage in both hands and opened up the Yellow Pages in search of a loan office. I dressed carefully for my errand, drove downtown to a small three- or four-story building in a shabby section of New Orleans, and found my goal on the second floor.

I entered the small office and asked to see the boss. When I had gained entrance to that person's cubbyhole, I found myself nervously explaining that I needed to borrow three hundred dollars, and could he let me have it?

The man was very kind to me, although he must have found my presence in his office somewhat bizarre. First he asked me what collateral I was prepared to put up. I had never even heard the word, so had to ask him to explain collateral to me. When he did, I told him that I didn't have any of those things. So what did my husband do? he wanted to know, and after asking me my maiden name, he asked if I was related to my grandfather, a prominent businessman in New Orleans. "Yes," I replied, "I'm his granddaughter." The loan agent's demeanor changed visibly.

After that everything was easy, and for the rest of the day and night I congratulated myself on having solved the problem. But this joy lasted only until the following day, as by then the loan office had contacted my father. It was an angry man who called to tell me never to do such a thing again, that he would go to the loan office that morning and clear my debt. All of this left me with confused feelings about men and life in general. How to know the right course to take? How to know whom to please?

Now I was in trouble with my parents, and, as I had not told Ted what I planned to do, begged my father not to say anything about it. Pleasing my husband was more important than pleasing my family, and so, fortunately or not, Ted never became aware of my efforts to hide my first "business dealings."

After this, my father insisted on giving me an allowance, and so Ted and I remained out of debt.

***

We rented a small apartment for a couple of years until we could build a house. I got pregnant in that apartment after experiencing an early miscarriage, which obliged me to spend most of the time in bed for the first three months of my next pregnancy. The miscarriage was very traumatic for me, needless to say. I had awakened in the middle of the night lying in a pool of blood. I crept quietly out of bed, so as not to disturb Ted, went into the bathroom where the unformed fetus slipped out of me and into the toilet. I returned to the bedroom, woke Ted, and asked him to call my doctor. The doctor told Ted to give me two aspirin and he would be over to see me in the morning.

I was told to wait for some months before trying again to get pregnant, and when I did it was to conceive my son. This time all went well and our son Teddy was born. This was a happy time for me, and when the baby was brought to me to be fed, I counted my blessings as I lay in bed between my husband and my son.

Not long ago I was with a group of people who were discussing the subject of happiness. Had we ever experienced it? If so, when? How? Is it an emotion which can be defined?, etc. There is a picture in my mind of a moment long ago when I was consciously aware of pure joy. My son was then about three and Ted's parents had brought him a little bright red blazer from Paris. I happened to glance out of the window in my bedroom down to the sidewalk below, and as I did so I saw Teddy and the nursemaid walking by. The child broke into a little skipping dance and it seemed such a joyous expression of his feelings that the joy transmitted itself to me and I consciously thought, "I'm happy right this instant!" I've had more than a few such moments during my lifetime, and consider each a real blessing.

Morning sickness was unknown to me, but when I came into the apartment on one hot day to be greeted by the strong odor of boiling shrimp, I was instantly aware that pregnancy had some drawbacks. My cook was preparing the shrimp to use in a dish that night for dinner, and it appeared to me that the whole world stank of shrimp. This was long before the day of air-conditioning, and it really was years before I could again enjoy those delicious crustaceans.

The same thing happened with turkey, another favorite which I was obliged to forego for some time, and aside from the awful time when I threw up in the dining room of the large summer hotel on the top of Lookout Mountain in Tennessee, I was relatively free of that unpleasant aspect of having a baby.

I was midway in my pregnancy when the aforementioned event occurred. With our closest friends, Ted and I had been spending a couple of weeks in the mountains of North Carolina at an unpretentious little resort. Our chief entertainments at Linville, outside watching an elderly gentleman with a fly swatter muttering to himself as each fly was dispatched, were leisurely golf and bridge, bridge, bridge. All of us were good players so time never hung heavily on our hands.

I went from Linville directly to Chattanooga to join my parents who were staying at the hotel while watching their new house being built. The first night I was there, the three of us sat quietly enjoying our meal, when with no warning I became violently ill. I was rooted to the spot. There was no chance to move: it was as if my legs were paralyzed and I was helpless. My mother reached into her water glass to fish out some ice that she rubbed on my wrists. Why, I don't know, maybe just to be doing something, anything. It was quite a scene, as can be imagined. Waiters came running with napkins. People stared. I was miserably embarrassed, but as soon as the episode was over I felt marvelous. If anything could be said to have been fortunate about that night, it was that our table was situated close to the door leading to the pantry, and it was through that door that I made my escape.

Finally Ted's and my beautiful new red-brick house with the white columns across the front and the fanlight over the white painted front door, was ready, ready in time for me to have my first child there. Just prior to his birth, as I sat straight up in bed, a position I had to sleep in, gasping for breath from a combination of an acute case of bronchitis and an imminent delivery, an older woman, a friend of my mother's, telephoned to ask me to serve on some board or committee.

I replied that as I was about to have a baby and was severely handicapped by having to struggle to breathe, I couldn't possibly do as she asked. To which she blithely insisted that of course I could, if not right then, in a month or so after the baby was born.

"Your grandmother and your mother have always been active in civic affairs, and we all expect that you will carry on the tradition." This woman went on to tell me that it was useless to ask help of those with nothing to do, as they never were able to find the time, but on the other hand, a man or woman who was already heavily involved would quite likely find he or she could fit it into an already full schedule. This, of course, is true, and her advice has proven useful to me throughout my life when I've needed to ask others for help.

That phone call may very well have started my career as an activist, both political and social, two roles I would later follow throughout my life. To say that I was intimidated by this forceful lady would be to understate the case. I was instantly plunged into guilt. After all, if they, Mother and Grandmother, had done those things, I mustn't let them down. The funny part is that on occasion I still let myself be intimidated by someone with a strong character who points out my obligations to me, but I am grateful that I was made aware at an early age of social and political responsibilities.

And so I began doing a certain amount of civic work, not much, and always for traditional causes, as I had not yet been introduced to a more radical way of thinking and being. That was to come many years later.

***

I had working for me as a butler at that time a young black man, and one bright but terrible Sunday afternoon in his life helped define my nature and certainly his as well.

It was the Sunday of his half-day off, and as it was a warm spring day he was wearing a white linen suit, then as doubtless now, dress-up wear for a man in the South. At that time practically all the help came from the black community and it was standard practice for them to go home at night. Their days off consisted of one half-day in midweek and every other Sunday the same. I well remember my shock when I found out that elsewhere in the country the help expected a whole day off each week with the same on alternate Sundays. "What would we eat?" I wondered in my naive, spoiled way, and that was the start of my learning to cook.

On this warm Sunday afternoon, I left Weldon waiting on the corner for the streetcar, smart in his Sunday whites. Half an hour or so went by before he returned to the house. His handsome light brown face was stricken, its color ashen. His so recently pristine white suit was now rumpled, stained, with bits of raw tomatoes clinging to it, and sticky egg yolk running down the front. This tall, good-looking young man was ruined, devastated, humiliated, and, I have always felt sure, marked for life on that day.

As he had stood waiting on the corner a car full of white hoodlums drove past. On seeing a black man standing there they began yelling and shouting, drove around the corner, and, returning, took out their ammunition and pelted him with raw eggs and tomatoes, then left him standing there alone, crucified.

He moved here to Santa Barbara some years ago. I shall miss him when he dies. He is one of the oldest friends I have in the world, and many memories are centered around Weldon. One of his endearing traits was his way of offering a drink. "Would you like a nice cold drink of water?" he would ask, or a nice hot cup of coffee if the day were cold, stressing always the adjective as if to make the offering more appealing. He always referred to a ladle as "lead," and when passing a silver gravy boat filled with hot gravy always warned the person he was serving to "be careful, the lead is very hot." As silver absorbs heat, of course his warning was timely.

Weldon's self-esteem has been low all his life. His first wife, Hilda, one of the dearest women I have known, used to say of him, "Poor Weldon doubts himself." The thoughtless cruelty of those unknown men of so long ago changed forever the lives of two people, Weldon's and mine.

My own social conscience had been activated by the presence in our house of the cook's little grandson Henry, and now and forever more was added another burden. I speak advisedly of a "burden," as for those of us who suffer vicariously, such happenings always add to our own suffering. Perhaps this is why we are compelled throughout our lives to go to the aid of others.

CHAPTER SEVEN

Falling In Love With Warren

*in love with the desert
a shiny new life*

I FIRST MET WARREN TREMAINE at the old Biltmore Hotel pool in Santa Barbara. I was living in New Orleans, married to Ted Simmons, and at that time was recovering from amoebic dysentery. I was just out of the hospital when my sister-in-law, Margaret, suggested I join her and her two small daughters for a vacation at the Miramar Hotel in Santa Barbara. I agreed with enthusiasm, engaged a nurse to come with us to care for my then five-year old son, and took off for Southern California to begin what was to be an enormous change in my life.

The year was 1935, before the Coral Casino was built, when the daily buffet luncheons around the Biltmore's swimming pool included swordfish and salmon when in season, barbecued daily along with steaks and ribs, and the elegant buffet was set out on long tables on the grass surrounding the pool. It was an attractively informal scene, and many of us who were there at that time deplored the coldness of the Casino when it was subsequently built.

My sister-in-law had arrived some time before I had. Having met quite a few people, Margaret invited me to lunch at the pool the day following my arrival to introduce me to her new friends. Since Warren was a young bachelor, Margaret had asked him to join us. I found him extremely attractive from the beginning and was delighted when he called the next day to ask if I would join him at the polo match that afternoon.

Warren dressed well in the casual way of an affluent man. He leaned towards tweed jackets and slacks, and didn't bother with a tie if he felt so inclined. He sometimes wore jeans or chinos, a dress pant for Western cattlemen, and always, to my eyes at least, looked devastatingly handsome.

He was lean, an inch or so over six feet, had straight brown hair that he assured me was really blond, and hazel eyes. Warren's sister-in-law, Dorothy, his older brother's first wife, joked about going to his tailors with him to "supervise" his fittings. In the ensuing years this job fell to me, and I sat through hours of advising him on patterns, textures, etc., although he always knew what he wanted.

Dorothy and Warren were great friends. He told me once that he considered her his best friend. Along with other provincial ideas, I had always felt that women had women friends, men had men friends. So this surprised me, just as I was surprised when Warren told me of another brother who had been in various businesses. In New Orleans where I had grown up and lived, most of the men I knew went into business with their fathers, the business having been founded perhaps by their grandfathers. The prevailing philosophy was "What was good enough for grandfather is good enough for me." I could never buy that philosophy. What was good enough for my grandfather wasn't nearly good enough for me. To reach out for the new, the untried, has been my way of life.

In addition to his good looks, Warren was a cattle rancher in Arizona, played polo, flew his own plane, and, as I was soon to discover, was already a full-fledged alcoholic. I was probably by then also a confirmed enabler. I had already experienced my father's alcoholism, my brother's, my first husband's, as well as that of several friends, so possibly I instantly recognized another . . . and unwittingly began enabling.

I always sensed Warren's vulnerability. I saw an actor on TV recently who appeared—as he walked away from the camera—to be holding pain between his shoulders. I thought immediately of Warren whose walk always suggested pain held in. I never lost the feeling that he was a helpless person who really needed someone to look after him.

Once during that first summer when we met, he and I, along with Margaret and two or three others drove down to Los Angeles to go to a nightclub and spend the night at the old Ambassador Hotel on Wilshire Boulevard. Even on that night, when Warren was forcibly ejected from the nightclub by two formidably large and determined bouncers, even then I overlooked and forgave his drinking. His crime was happiness, which manifested itself in exuberant cowboy yells. He sat at our table, drunk and happy, and every now and then gave a piercing "Yip! Yip! Yip!" as if he were on a horse chasing a bunch of cattle down an arroyo on the Tremaine ranch in Northern Arizona. The only trouble was that this scenario was only in his handsome and befuddled head.

I sat with him in the car while we waited for the others to join us, and believe me all sorts of thoughts ran through my head. His alcoholism devastated me and yet, whenever I saw him walking towards me, it was as if something endearing passed between us and pierced my heart.

I had begun that mysterious process known as falling in love. My grandmother laughed when she heard that Warren, too, was recovering from amoebic dysentery. She said she had heard of many reasons for people falling in love, but diarrhea was a new one to her.

We all drove home in light-hearted spirits the next day as if nothing had happened to interfere with our evening. The Conspiracy of Silence was working well and cloaked the nightclub incident.

***

Our pleasant daily routine continued through the following weeks. By the time I was due to return to New Orleans, Ted had come to California only to be told by me that his life had been turned upside down because Warren had proposed to me and I had accepted.

My marriage to Ted had gone steadily downhill for many reasons. Needless to say, the fact that he never had brought me to orgasm was a major consideration. Speaking with my mother one day on the subject of my marriage, not much more than a year after it had taken place, I confessed to her that, as far as I was concerned, if I never saw my husband again it would be alright with me. My mother was shocked to hear this, and of course this may be why I expressed it so forcibly to her, just for the fact of shocking her. At any rate, I was to experience great interest in two more men. With me, at that period in my life, it was a case of "How happy I could be with either, were t'other dear charmer away." And is it possible at nineteen, when I married Ted, to know what you really want, or need? In fact, it has always seemed to me a miracle if two people do manage to choose the right partner for life. I can't imagine both people growing simultaneously and in the same direction as the other. Or should we simply recognize the fact of incompatibility and hang on as best we can?—which is what most people do, of course.

When Warren took me to dinner one night at the Biltmore, and almost casually suggested that I divorce Ted and marry him, somehow it didn't seem strange to be accepting a proposal of marriage while still married to another man. Ted was almost in the category of being married to business and common interests with his men friends. The interests that we shared were bridge and golf, and of course when our son was born, he was a bridge between us. Ted, however, whenever I asked his intervention in disciplining Teddy, always said it was my responsibility until he was fourteen and after that he would take over.

Poor Ted. He had come to spend what was to have been ten days with his wife and son, enjoying his own vacation and found instead that his life had been forever altered by a man he had never seen. That was a time of anguish of another sort not only for Ted, but for me as well. I don't remember ever doing anything more difficult.

In fact, I have no recollection of actually telling Ted of my decision to leave him, marry Warren and live in Arizona. I have struggled all my life to be more tactful, to be able to express myself without hurting another, but have on many occasions failed. I have blocked that painful scene out so well that it is totally gone from my memory. I remember taking him down to the train station in Santa Barbara, putting him on the train, then driving back to the Miramar along the waterfront, stopping the car and sitting there sobbing.

Of course, my very genuine grief was tempered by the fact of being in love and knowing that soon I would be with Warren. He had left Santa Barbara before Ted arrived, and was to return that night, so my pain would soon be lessened. I felt great grief because of inflicting pain on my husband, who liked the status quo and had no wish to change it, but I also felt tremendous relief to know that I had actually made the break.

I have to confess that the fact that Warren was rich played a small but real part in my feelings for him. It isn't easy to make this confession, as I have already written critically about my mother's materialistic nature, but I now realize that I was equally materialistic at that time of my life. Being myself wealthy, I saw that Warren and

I would have an easy, pleasant life. Affluence attracts affluence. Our lives would be rich in everything that money could buy, as well as a few things that it couldn't.

My mother, on hearing the news that I had decided to divorce Ted and marry Warren Tremaine, reacted with conventional disapproval and spoke as if I were ten years old rather than twenty-seven. "Of course, you're going to do nothing of the kind. Come upstairs with me and we'll discuss it."

Docilely, I followed her up the broad staircase into her bedroom, but I assured her that I was going to do just what I had said I would. Her advice to me was to do as the French do, and I quote, "Keep the marriage intact and take a lover if you must, but keep the family together." But Warren and Arizona were beckoning, and I knew where I wanted my future to lie.

Warren's father, it must be noted, was just as horrified as my mother. He himself had been through a divorce from his first wife in the very late part of the nineteenth century. Although I never knew any details of this happening, it undoubtedly colored his feelings about divorce. He didn't like the idea that it was his son who had broken up a marriage, even though I assured him that the marriage had been shaky for a long time.

So my mother and I boarded the train one chilly October night in New Orleans for the trip up through the southeastern part of the country to New York, the neutral meeting ground on which we had decided for a conference between the parents. I felt somewhat embarrassed by this whole thing. After all, I was a married woman and a mother. I was accustomed to making my own decisions and thought it ludicrous to have our parents talking over our lives as if we were teenagers. To Warren it wasn't as strange as it was to me. His mother had died when he was three years old, and as he was the youngest of his father's six children, he was in real awe of his formidable father. Father Tremaine was a man prominent in Eastern business and financial circles, much as my grandfather was, and to be frank I was a bit awed by him myself, as I had been by Pere.

I never really knew what transpired between my mother and Warren's father at their meeting, but on the surface at least it was a satisfactory one. My mother could charm the birds off of the trees when she wanted to, and I imagine that she did not waste that talent.

Feeling like a child who has just received parental approval for a dubious project, I set off for Reno and six weeks of waiting. I made a few friends, including a young lawyer . . . not mine . . . who proposed to me and told me he would take me to Hawaii for a honeymoon. I thanked him, and said that was where Warren was taking me.

That incident made me remember that a short time before my marriage to Ted, Fran Blom, a Danish archaeologist, who headed the department of Middle American History at Tulane University and who was considerably older than I, invited me to have lunch and proceeded to beg me to call off my forthcoming wedding, and marry him instead. This very charming man was, it turned out, another alcoholic. This was the first indication I had that he was in love with me, although I had

been out with him several times and enjoyed his company very much. I wonder now, all these years later,
could he have spotted the "enabler" quality in me? He
was a delightful man, and although his middle years were
filled with tragedy resulting from his alcoholism, I heard
that later on he had made a wonderful recovery and
finished his life with distinction.

***

I had a pleasant enough time in Reno. I rode horseback every afternoon, read a lot, listened to music,
walked by the river, and enjoyed the little black cocker
spaniel Warren had flown up to me from Phoenix.
Finally I had my decree and left for Arizona, flying down
in Warren's plane which he had sent up with a pilot. For
some reason it didn't seem quite right for me to leave
with my lover, but alright in my lover's plane.

It was an afternoon in late December. We were late
in getting off from Reno in Warren's small four-seater
single motor plane. Once in the air, we bounced around
that cold December sky for hours. Finally the pilot
confessed to me that he had no idea where we were. The
plane was equipped with blind-flying mechanism and
while Warren understood and used it, this pilot did not.
He told me at last that he would drop down close to the
earth to see if he could get a bearing as to where we were.
He did this and I saw immediately that we were in Death
Valley. Three days prior to this I had received a postcard
depicting Scotty's Castle, and there it was just below us.

The pilot was relieved, as was I, and we spent the night in Las Vegas, flying on to Scottsdale the following morning.

I stayed a few days there before returning to New Orleans. I had followed the advice of both my mother and my mother-in-law in not telling my small son that I was divorcing his father before going to Reno. I regret it to this day and strongly advise truth at all times. He was a very unhappy little boy and, to make matters worse, his cousin, just his age, had told him while I was away that he would never see me again. I stayed in New Orleans over the holidays, then returned to Arizona leaving my son with his father, and assuring him that he would be coming out to join us in a few weeks.

Warren and I had decided on a date in February 1935 for our wedding. We looked up a justice of the peace, invited my sister-in-law, Margaret, who happened to be in California, and had a morning wedding at his eldest brother's house in Westwood. The only other guests were Carl and his wife at that time, and a chauffeur from a limousine service who was known to Warren and who was to take us to the docks where the Lurline was docked. We went straight down to the boat to find champagne and hors d'oeuvres waiting in our stateroom. A champagne life awaited us, it seemed.

A few alarming incidents occurred while we were on our honeymoon, in Honolulu, and on the boat going down to the islands and returning some weeks later, enough to show me that I had married a man who really liked to drink. There were times when I was embarrassed, not only for my new husband but for myself as well. There was no fooling around when he got started, but being the enabler I am, it wasn't too hard to rationalize, and as I am an optimist by nature, I found ways to be hopeful for our future.

The night before we were to dock in Los Angeles, our cabin steward poured Warren into our room in the early light of dawn. Needless to say, we had a bit of trouble getting him off the boat the following day. He had cabled Carl, the pilot who had flown me down from Reno, to bring his plane to Los Angeles from Phoenix. His brother met us at the boat, and after we had stumbled somehow through lunch, we drove out to the airport, met Carl, and took off, supposedly for Phoenix. Palm Springs was as far as we got, however. It was evident that Warren needed sleep more than anything else. Carl and I had dinner together, and I then went to bed. Somewhere around three in the morning Warren woke me to say he was hungry, and would I go with him to get something to eat. When he had been very drunk, "drunk out of his mind" as the saying used to be, I always had the feeling that he had returned from a trip, and of course, in a very real way he had done just that.

We found a fast food place where Warren ate his first meal probably since lunch time the day before. I remember thinking . . . what a way to end a honeymoon! sitting in a dingy restaurant with a husband who didn't really know where he was yet. Pathetic.

Yet we had fun! For me just to be on the desert, to be where I could see a hundred miles to mountain peaks with no obstructions in the way, where I could smell the desert smells and feel the magic of the desert silence, these experiences made each day a wondrous new world. I enjoyed everything about ranch life that I had heard from Warren, and I knew it was what I had been longing for.

We drove up to the Tremaine Ranch in the first autumn of our marriage to experience some quail shooting, and I was ecstatic. The main ranch house where we generally stayed was closed, as Warren's parents had gone back east for the winter, so we stayed in the bunk house with the cowboys. Another first for me! When we arrived at the ranch in the evening, the men had just butchered a calf, and if you have never eaten a freshly killed piece of beef, even a young and presumably tender calf, let me explain that you could as well be chewing on the table's edge. It was my initial experience with the subject of tenderizing meat. In New Orleans I had bought steaks, chops, and so on at the meat market with never a thought as to how long the beef had been hanging. Now I knew differently. But it was what we had for dinner that night, for breakfast the following morning, along with eggs and pancakes, and certainly for at least one more meal before we went back down to the desert. It was exciting for me to be living that way. The only light we had was from oil lamps, and the only toilet facilities were outside. During our first night there I had to get up during the night, and you can imagine that it took courage to get out of a warm bed next to a warm husband and run outside to the outhouse, but the night was so beautiful, the stars so close in the clear Arizona sky, that it more than compensated for the cold, crisp air.

A mink coat is lovely and luxurious, but first-class travel on enormous luxury liners isn't really all that much fun. Riding with the cowboys on an all-day round-up was more to my taste, and finding myself deep into the mountains, seeing range after range, was the most exciting thing that ever happened to me. Having been Rex's Queen was pale beside this!

Warren had taken me into Phoenix shortly after we returned from our honeymoon and supervised my exciting cowboy purchases. This was what I had yearned for all my life. Being in a Western town, then a small Western town in a huge state that boasted less than half a million people, was my dream come true.

We ordered a Western saddle to be made to my measurements, leather chaps likewise, cowboy boots, and a twenty-gauge shotgun! Although I may have looked like a city slicker dressed up in cowboy clothes, in my imagination I was a ranch woman, a ranch woman with a ranch woman's responsibilities. In reality that was what I wanted to be. Only a few years later we came close to buying a cattle ranch, a beautiful spread adjoining the Tremaines' Bar T Bar ranch, in the high country of northern Arizona. But, as it happened, by that time the Coral Casino had been built in Montecito, and Warren preferred life in Montecito and the Casino to the wilderness of northern Arizona.

So the die had been cast for us. We were forever caught in the tenderness of the trap that was Montecito life.

I believe that Warren's drinking allowed him to relax and actually have times of happiness. He was not a happy man ever, and his appearance showed this, but when he was drunk he could laugh, he could dance, he could do all of the things he really must have yearned to do but was too inhibited to permit himself the luxury of doing.

CHAPTER EIGHT

The Wild West

silence . . . space
and blazing sun
my dream come true

LIFE IN ARIZONA when Warren and I first were married was full of joyous experiences. Having always yearned for a life with space and sky around me, now here it was, not a myth, not a longing, but here and now.

Every day I woke up to sun and song. Birds were everywhere on the desert, and at once my heart was sweetly pierced, as it is today, by the plaintive call of the mourning dove.

I had never even held a gun in my former life, much less shot one, but now I did and came perilously close to shooting a friend one afternoon. We sometimes went out to nearby fields in the late afternoon to catch the doves' evening flight. The evening flight meant that the birds were returning to their roosting place, so that was a good time to shoot them. Imagine such cruelty. While the men were close by waiting for the birds to come over, I

111

was sitting talking with a friend who chose to quietly sew while waiting for her husband.

Suddenly Warren called to me in a low voice that the birds were approaching. I got up hurriedly and to my horror my gun went off towards the other side of the clearing where Barbara was sitting. I was so new to this that I had sat unthinkingly with the gun across my lap, without the safety catch as we idly talked. Nothing happened, Barbara was not hit, but I was scared silly and learned a valuable lesson. I must repeat that I can't imagine myself shooting birds today, but in my wish to please my husband I did just that.

To anyone who knows Phoenix today, it will seem incredible to be told that it was a small Western town in 1936, a small town surrounded by miles and miles of citrus orchards which, when flowering in the spring, saturated the entire Salt River Valley with the intoxicating fragrance of orange blossoms.

I liked my new friends, new life, and I was instantly enthralled by the desert's spell. I was enchanted by my new husband's stories of his friends, particularly one who was, like himself, newly married.

Louis Sands lived in a town on the west side of Phoenix which meant that when we drove over for a visit with him and his wife, it was a matter of twenty-five or thirty miles. I am now getting used to this again, living part-time as I do in the sparsely settled southwest corner of New Mexico, but at that time, coming straight from city life, such long drives to visit a friend seemed very strange.

These two reckless young men found themselves from time to time waking in the same room, either Warren's or his friend's. Warren told me that he had on one occasion awakened to the sound of his friend, sitting half up in bed and leaning on his elbow, shooting at his boots across the room. When asked why, he explained that he thought there might be scorpions in them and wanted to scare them out before putting the boots on.

Louis drank a great deal but only the cheapest whiskey. I have a picture of him that is as clear in my mind as if it had happened last week. He is sitting on the sofa in our living room gulping hard, giving every indication that he is trying not to throw up. He is tall—six feet four or five—a skinny cowboy, and there he sits, legs stretched out before him, an empty shot glass in one hand and a look of utter horror on his face. Louis had asked for a drink and William, our butler, a prankster himself with that strange British humor, had brought him a decanter with the good whiskey rather than the one we kept just for Louis. I was really nervous. Our house was newly built, newly decorated, and the rug in front of our guest was, I feared, in imminent danger. As it turned out, my fears were groundless and I always wondered if William deliberately switched the decanters just to see the effect.

One balmy winter afternoon after Sunday lunch we sat on the screened porch having coffee with our guests. The guests included some people we hadn't met before, friends of friends, people on whom I wanted to make a good impression. Sitting there, playing what a friend

used to call a "lady-come-to-see" role, the air was suddenly filled with a horrendous, chaotic noise. Across the
lawn in front of us came our butler, William. He had
removed his dark grey morning coat and over his white
shirt and striped trousers he was wearing a white apron.
A comic rubber mask covering his head was representing
a black man and he was trailed by some thirteen dogs.
Besides four cocker spaniels we had a beautiful boxer
bitch who recently had produced eight fine pups. William had a whistle in his mouth with which he communicated with the thirteen dogs as they tore across the
lawn in front of us. He was running as fast as he could,
as were the dogs, tumbling over each other, and all
barking like crazy. It was a scene from a madhouse and I
was mortified. I wasn't secure enough in myself not to
worry about what the guests of honor would think, but
everyone of course thought it hilarious.

William and his wife, Carrie, were with us for
seventeen years. We thought of them as a part of ourselves, our family. Our children regarded them as grandparents, and both Carrie and William considered our
children as their own grandchildren. Those two people
are involved in my most cherished memories. I was
incredibly fortunate to have them in my life. Carrie was
a really fine cook, having had early training in some fine
houses in London, and William's eccentricities were
more than balanced by his many talents. He had spent
fourteen of his young years in the British navy where the
men did their own tailoring, resoled shoes, tinkered with
machines, and in general learned a multitude of skills.
We never called a plumber, electrician, or workman of

any sort without William first trying his hand at the job and generally fixing it. I was truly blessed by those two, and I appreciated them enormously.

***

One of the greatest aspects of my new life in Arizona was the unbelievable feeling of freedom.

All the world was flooded with sunshine from the time I got up in the morning to the end of the day when Warren and I would be together again. I had finally found out what Lady Chatterly and all the others had been so ecstatic about and, our sex life was really good.

There was a light-hearted joyousness about those early years in Arizona. Blue and gold and the pinkish tan of the desert pervaded my life. There were the beautiful mountains ringing the Salt River Valley in the background, and over everything the silence of the desert.

Warren's work schedule was hardly taxing. It usually consisted of a quick trip over to the Mesa ranch headquarters to check out how things were going and then returning home to lunch with me. The Mesa portion of the ranch consisted of a section of land lying between Mesa and Chandler, two small towns back in those days, about twenty-five miles from where we lived on the desert near Scottsdale.

Warren's father was a well-known and highly respected senior vice-president of General Electric. He lived in Cleveland where he had established Nela Park, one of the first corporate think tanks in the country. NELA Park, incidentally, stood for National Electric

Lamp Association. He had built this desert oasis not only for himself and his family to enjoy, but to entertain business friends and colleagues as well. The residential part consisted of a compound of small white cottages all on an impeccably kept green lawn. Each member of the family who spent much time there had his or her own cottage. These small white dwellings with their green roofs were scattered over a large lawn with Warren's parents' house pretty well isolated from the compound. In close proximity to the crystal clear swimming pool were the dining room and kitchen in one house and the playroom—a large single room in another house with strikingly beautiful Navajo rugs spread here and there on polished floors.

The power lines were buried underground. It was the first time I had seen that, as to burying power lines at that time was an unusual, almost radical step, and to achieve this expensive, uncluttered effect created a welcome sight. The residence compound was surrounded by bright green alfalfa fields. Generally cattle could be seen feeding in the fields, and in the fall when the calves had been taken from their mothers, to be sent to feed lots for fattening, the air resounded with the plaintive and heartbreaking bawling of the cows and calves trying to find each other.

The feed lot, the reason for the ranch operation, was as far as possible from the residence section. I was told the story about a frantic night years before when the cattle stampeded. Many were mangled beneath the wheels of the Southern Pacific passenger train barreling through Arizona on its way to New Orleans. Lawsuits flew about for a long time. Much damage was done to the train itself, and all train schedules were held up for hours while the tracks and cars of the train were repaired. Even as far up the driveway as the residential area, cattle stumbled around all night, tearing up the lawn, soiling all the walkways, and some may even have fallen into the pool.

The Bar T Bar ranch, at that time headquartered in the Tonto Basin of Zane Grey fame, was a cow ranch where the cows and calves roamed the hilly range with a few herd bulls among them. It was a totally different operation from the Mesa Ranch down in the Salt River Valley which existed only to feed and fatten the cattle. Ten thousand head could be handled in those feed lots. I appreciated the sounds of lowing cows and even the smells of same.

An interesting fact about the cattle industry was that it was more profitable to sell the cattle during, or just after the full moon, because in the bright moonlight they would eat all night long, adding considerably to their weight, which in turn added considerably to their value. Range cattle would be brought into the feed lot right from the cow ranches to be fattened for sale to the lucrative Los Angeles market.

I remember one small man who walked with a severe limp. He was the brother of a well-known band leader and also was a cattle buyer. This was when I first began to know people very different from myself or anyone I had ever known.

Some six or seven years ago, in the early eighties, I had occasion to spend a night at the Adams Hotel in

Phoenix. To my disappointment, I found that it now looks just like every other hotel in America, all of the charm and space of its early years gone. Back in those days the lobby had been huge. The high ceiling had exposed the mezzanine floor with its open corridor overlooking the lobby below. Comfortable sofas and chairs were plentiful, as well as low tables complete with ashtrays and daily papers. The occupants of the furniture dressed in jeans, well-worn boots, ten-gallon hats, and fancy cowboy shirts. When they got to the dining room they all ordered Cattleman's Cuts, thick steaks cut so high that they resembled enormous slices of roast beef. I tried these out but found them to be too heavy for me.

***

Shortly after Warren and I had returned from our honeymoon in Hawaii, we had occasion to drive with Boss Chilson, the ranch foreman, up to northern Arizona. Boss was a wonderful man, and knowing him was a privilege I look back on with fond pleasure. Boss had been a cow rancher in Arizona for many years, as had his father before him. He was greatly respected throughout the entire state, as much for his wonderful personality as for his undoubted knowledge of the cattle business.

For the benefit of readers unfamiliar with ranch terminology, a cow ranch is one where a herd of cows is kept along with a few bulls, the purpose being to breed the cows and eventually sell the calves. On a large ranch, hours can be spent during a roundup, often with the appearance that only a few head have been found, but it is not so. I have heard Boss at the start of the day give an order for so-and-so to ride up into such-and-such canyon and "bring down that old cow that nobody's seen for years. She'll have two or three calves with her by now." Sure enough it would happen just that way. The designated cowboy would find her and, wild as she was by then, would get her and her offspring to follow him some way. At day's end he would lead them peace-fully back to headquarters to join the rest of us, each group coming in with a few head to merge into a bunch, by then maybe fifty or sixty head of milling, bawling cattle.

The purpose of our trip was to talk to a couple of men who were interested in buying a part of the cattle ranch in that portion of the state, as it was proving economically unsound to the whole operation.

After leaving the low desert area around Phoenix, we climbed steadily northeast into the mountains. After a few hours of driving we stopped along the main road by a gate. Behind the gate a dirt road led up to the small ranch house where one of the potential buyers lived. He must have been watching for us as he soon ambled down the road to where we waited, whereupon Warren and Boss got out of the car to greet him and commence negotiations.

I maintained a respectful distance in the back seat of the car, not wanting to be interfering. To a woman accustomed to men who led nine-to-five lives, this was beautiful. The three men stood by the fence, all similarly dressed in well-worn jeans, boots, and big hats, one chewing on a blade of grass, one on a wad of tobacco, all talking in low tones and smiling easily as they spoke. They leaned their elbows on the top of the fence, propped one foot up on the lowest rail, and gave every evidence of enjoying themselves in the freshness of the morning. It always seemed to me as if ranchers enjoyed their lives a great deal.

After a suitable time passed, the conversation began to wind down, notes were taken and stuffed into pockets, and goodbyes were said. Warren and Boss returned to the car, and we were off to the next man. We stopped at a small settlement along the way where we bought food at the combination gas-and-grocery store before we proceeded on to our next potential buyer.

This time we pulled off to the side of the road at the head of a long, deep canyon and after waiting for some time, our man finally appeared. He was mounted on a mule and was climbing slowly up the steep sides of the canyon from his own ranch down in the very bottom.

Talk about fascinating! Here was this well-worn, past middle-aged rancher (who turned out to be the eventual buyer), keeping his appointment with us at the head of his canyon, talking terms with Warren and Boss, and finalizing the deal all by the side of the road in the heart of the Arizona White Mountains. The price of this ranch was not exactly peanuts, I must add, but still this man could afford to pay cash. It heartens my soul to know that this sort of business still goes on all over the world. A nice change from lawyers, accountants, computers, and the high-tech world we see around us every day.

We ended that day at our ranch headquarters, a small cabin occupied by the one rancher who was responsible for that part of the operation. He welcomed us and introduced us to two others who had dropped by to seek hospitality. There was one other rancher and an old miner who needed shelter. They were just about to sit down to supper and invited us to join them. There was a small bedroom with the rest of the house, one big room, sitting room, eating place, etc., so our host offered the bedroom with its one bed to Warren and me. I was new to such casual arrangements and welcomed his offer. We put our sleeping bags on the bed, didn't take off much clothing, as it was really cold by now, and had a moderately comfortable night. This house had no plumbing, to be sure, so it meant more cold trips outside, but that was alright, since by now I was getting used to this ranch routine.

The next morning was a real test. Since we were at such a high altitude it was a pretty crisp morning to wake up to. The men were as before, courteous and considerate, so they all went outside and stomped around in the cold while we dressed in front of the huge fire in the big room. Everyone was rewarded with a breakfast before we dispersed for the day.

Boss, Warren, and I spent that day on the ranch, which gave me a chance to see more beautiful country. I never met a mean-spirited cowboy while I was in Arizona. All, with no exceptions, were good people to be with, friendly, open, always ready with help or advice for a novice, truly wonderful to know, and I really appreciated them. I believe that living in peaceful wilderness surroundings contribute to the easy-going natures of the people I got to know during my years in Arizona.

***

On another occasion we went with a few others over to the Meteor Crater, which is on the Tremaine ranch and is said to be the largest on the planet. The first teams of astronauts were taken there for training and afterwards a museum was built on the edge; it is a popular tourist attraction. As I remember, Warren's older brother was there, along with Boss's elder son and his wife. We stood on the edge of the crater talking of various things. There was no development at all then, only the naturally majestic aspects of the crater, a magnificent and awesome sight. As we stood there we watched a gathering storm approaching. Huge clouds billowed up from below the horizon, darkening as they raced towards us, and it was clear that we were in for a real storm. We were standing close to a clump of juniper trees and moved away from them so as not to be hit by the lightning that is common with desert storms. Just in time too, as suddenly the thunder crashed over our heads and the sky was split by jagged flashes. The lightning cracked open a huge boulder about five or six feet from where I stood, and I literally felt and tasted the electricity in every one of the gold fillings in my teeth.

CHAPTER NINE

Me As Mom

after the babies
what to do . . .
I need my own life

I WONDER WHY IT HAS ALWAYS BEEN SO HARD for me to be a mother. I actually enjoyed the process of "making a baby," as I have heard conception described, but when the baby arrived, my own life intruded and I wanted someone else to care for it.

Often I resented the time I was obliged to be with a child, especially during the World War II period. Warren thought it was unnatural for a mother to be bored with her children, but I strongly doubt that I was the only one to have had that feeling. I found I had no patience with, nor enjoyment of, endless paper-doll talk.

However I learned a lot from my children during this time. My room looked out on the back yard, with windows wide open to the balmy Arizona weather, and I frankly enjoyed eavesdropping. Children reveal themselves better when no grownups are around, and I was being taught all the time. I was helpless in the kitchen, and I knew next to nothing about dusting and sweeping, but I was learning about human nature from my children.

I confess that I am not much better now . . . at cooking, yes, but not at cleaning. It seems I wasn't cut out to be a housewife in the domestic sense of the word. I needed independence and freedom rather than the slow pace of being at home with the children waiting for Warren to come home. Yet at times I have wished I were that woman.

Committing to mothering would have resulted in a very different life from the one I chose. I wanted to get up with the dawn, go to the racetrack still misty with the night's fog, and watch the horses work out. It was exciting standing close to the fence by the starting gate. I could hear the shouts, the commands, the curses, see the often frightened horses rearing and plunging in their stalls, and then the earth-shaking thunder of hooves only a few feet from where I stood. I enjoyed every minute of it. Afterwards we would go over to the employees' dining room and have breakfast while visiting with the trainers and jockeys. At the cattle ranch in northern Arizona owned by Warren's family, riding with the cowboys on all-day roundups was wonderful, too. And to be on the water all day . . . whether the Pacific Ocean or the Sea of Cortez, or maybe best of all a day fishing a trout stream in a quiet countryside, I loved all of those experiences and a thousand others too. But I must confess, I never loved staying at home with the babies.

I am avoiding the real issue of mothering: I never was very good at it, and I still don't know why. The very words, mothering, comforting, cuddling, cozy . . . those words make me uncomfortable when I say them. Closeness frightens me, with the exception of sexual closeness with a man I love. I am all too aware that this quality in my nature has been hard on my children, and hard on me as well. There exists between me and my children a barrier of sorts. I have held them at arms' length rather than enfolded them. Why? It is very hard to write about this, just as it is hard to write about the alcoholics in my family, and the cruelties I have knowingly perpetrated. In spite of being a strong woman, I have plenty of weaknesses.

I see couples who have been together for a long time and a sense of envy comes over me. I think it must be wonderful to come to the end of your days with a man you have known your entire life. A comfortable way to have lived. But that wouldn't have been for me. I wasn't meant to be that stay-at-home woman. I was meant instead to have many experiences, to know many people, to express many interests, and to come down to the wire, so to speak, with a pretty good record after all.

Other than thinking that my children could have had a better break in their lives had I been a more loving mother, I'm satisfied with my life. And I did, and do love my children very much.

***

I am lying on the chaise lounge in the corner of my bedroom where two windows form the corner. I have been reading and am interrupted by my son's running into my room to share his joy. For him it is the last day of school and the first of vacation. His ten-year-old face shines with happy anticipation.

For me it is a hot afternoon in late May on the Sonoran desert of southern Arizona. I am pregnant and feeling decidedly out of sorts with my world. Because of my verbal abuse, the child who bubbled with joy when he came to me from school was soon reduced to teary sobbing and meek apologizing. It didn't take long. Fifteen minutes was enough to change his joy to misery. Apologizing for what? I have no idea nor probably would he if I were to recall this scene to him. In my zeal to make things pleasant for my new husband, my new family really, as Diana was two years old then, and in a futile attempt to express my own frustration with the whole picture of my life, which included my growing awareness of Warren's alcoholism, I used my small son as a verbal target. Later on I did the same thing with the other children. I demanded my son be an adult. I expected him to react maturely to his life, which often must have caused him confusion and fear.

He secretly must have longed for his New Orleans home, for friends and family still there, for familiar surroundings, but he never complained, never let me see whatever unhappiness he had. His homesickness might have been overwhelming, but if it was, I never knew it.

This was not the only occasion on which I used him to express my unhappiness. It is all too easy to find a tiny chink in a child's armor, and having found it, to pry it ever more open until the breaking point is finally reached and either open rebellion or helpless acquiescence occurs.

My daughter Katy swears to this day that I pushed her down the cement cellar stairs of our Santa Barbara house, and although I as strongly insist that I did not, I do recall that I was very angry with her. I did take hold of her slender little shoulders and shake her hard, thereby possibly causing her to lose her balance and fall, as she did, to the very bottom of the long flight of stone stairs . . . and I walked away, leaving her cries behind me.

***

In 1943 Warren and I sold our big house on the desert and moved into a much smaller one on the outskirts of Phoenix. We bought the house just as it was, furniture and all, and it was certainly unlike any house I had lived in before or since. It was built in the middle of two-and-a-half acres of alfalfa, and was more or less Victorian in a Los Angeles way. It had obviously been furnished by a decorator. It was close to Central Avenue, the main street of Phoenix. It had a swimming pool with a small guest house next to it, and was in an area just being developed as residential. Gone were the bigger pieces of land, and in their place were houses, houses, and more houses.

This proximity to a main artery gave us all a good scare when Katy, then barely three, decided to run away from home. This occurred on a cold winter day, early in the morning when Diana was getting ready for school. I was sitting at the breakfast table in the bay window having a second cup of coffee. I don't recall the source of the controversy, but I clearly remember the picture of the child.

Carrie and William, our wonderful English cook and butler, had returned from Los Angeles and were once again making life comfortable for us. The meals were wonderful, I didn't have to make the beds, I could leave the house and live a normal life, and I was grateful! This day Katy came out of her room, struggling into her heavy coat, wearing a little wool cap, and without a word to any of us she opened the heavy front door and started off down the driveway.

Carrie, William, and I stood in the window watching the small figure marching down the long straight driveway to the street. I was frightened because when she reached the street she would have to turn left or right, and either way she would arrive at a busy street embroiled in the midst of morning rush-hour traffic. Carrie and William were frantic. Although I was equally worried, I felt we should let her go a bit farther, and, in the end, Katy won the battle. As she came closer and closer to the driveway's end, I had to give in and tell William that the time had come to end her journey. Down the driveway ran our dignified William to return with an armful of furious little girl.

At that point in my life I had always lived with servants, and consequently had very little knowledge of practical housekeeping. I didn't know how to cook, except for the brief times I ventured into the kitchen and tried my hand at cheesecakes and similar necessities of life. That is typical of me, now that I think about it. I never read the directions when using a new object. I prefer to leap ahead, as if I already understood the process. Rather than begin cooking with simple dishes, getting a little information as I went along, I started out with cheesecake. This became a family joke, and Warren and Teddy enjoyed telling about the days when all anyone in the family ate was cheesecake as that was my sole accomplishment.

I think this must have been a hard time for all of us. I know it was for me, and I know that as a consequence I was often impatient and handed out injustice as often as justice. Diana, the elder of the two girls, was six and in first grade. My son, Teddy, was a lean, lanky fourteen-year old working in a garage at the sort of job fourteen-year-olds work in the summertime.

For the novice cook and housekeeper, this is how my day went. I was up shortly after six, into the kitchen to start breakfast and back to my room trying to be quiet so as not to disturb my sleeping husband, who all of his life found it hard to rise before eleven. I brushed my teeth, showered, dressed, woke the girls, started them getting dressed, and returned to the kitchen to finish preparing breakfast. This routine included a few trips back to the girls' room to push them along their way. At last it was done, and as Teddy was up by then, the four of us would sit down to eat.

One afternoon I left the girls with a baby sitter and went into town. I returned just at the end of their nap period and was horrified to see the wall paper behind

Katy's bed covered with bright scrawly squiggles in many colors. Without even thinking I grabbed Katy up from her bed and spanked her. She began screaming. Diana jumped out of her bed, ran up behind me, and tried to bite my ankles all the while shouting at me to stop punishing Katy. It wasn't until years later that I learned that the wall decorations behind Katy's bed had been put there purposely as a surprise for me. Anyone who has ever been involved in a similar situation can imagine my shame and chagrin. I used to torture myself by imagining the dialogue leading up to the crayoning of the wall, something along the lines of "I'm going to do a surprise for Mummy, so when she comes home she'll see this beautiful picture." But Mummy turned into a she-devil when she saw the picture and never knew it was a surprise just for her.

***

Alas for the past, for the days when breakfast was brought to me on a tray, when Diana would come to my room to say goodbye before leaving for school and to ask if she and Lillian, the gardener's child, could each pick a navel orange (she pronounced it as one word) to take to school. During the long period of no help, when William and Carrie were still in California, if I heard the vacuum humming over the floors, I would be pushing it. If I wanted to hear the pulsing water in the washing machine, I had to do it . . . until Effie came into my life. Dear Effie! She was a lovely black lady who came to do our laundry, and talk with me as we sat in the kitchen eating the lunch I had just cooked. I loved Effie, and when I left for California a few years later, we hugged and kissed and cried because we had to separate.

I was exhausted by evening, and although I always promised myself each day that I would not cry when Warren asked me how my day had been, I never could keep that promise. I was not only tired, I felt very much alone. There was no one to help me and no prospects of finding anyone because everyone had gone into war work. I had never cleaned the bathtub or the toilet. I could push the broom around but I wasn't adept at sweeping up the dust. I didn't even know how to make a bed well, and disliked doing it besides. I couldn't remember where I had dusted and where I hadn't. I still don't know how to mop a floor or wring out the mop head.

I made lots of mistakes. I flew off the handle. I was bored. I wasn't used to spending my time with two little girls, even if they were my own, and the intellectual stimulation I was getting was nil. Warren told me that I was an unnatural mother to be so bored. Mothers were supposed to take care of their children, which of course cannot be denied, but this was a new way of living for me. As far as I was concerned, it left a lot to be desired.

Warren, like myself, had been brought up by servants. Although I had two husbands, neither of them could change a light bulb. Or, if they could, they kept it from me. It is painful to remember the scenes with Warren about picking up his clothes, his mail, his newspaper. His answer was always the same and was perfectly logical: "Pick it up yourself if it bothers you; it doesn't bother me."

The frustration I experienced was the same as I felt years later when we were driving down the Pacific Coast Highway to the race track. Warren wanted air-conditioning regardless of the temperature. If I wanted fresh air or to smell the sea perhaps, or to clear the smoke from the air inside the car, I opened the window by my seat. His method of control was simple: push the button that locked all the windows in the car, thereby making it impossible for me, or anyone else, to open a window unless he gave permission.

I know this time must have been very hard for Warren as well. He had never worked at any of the things he was now doing and it took a toll on his health. Certainly he wasn't used to the meals he was now being served. I don't have any way of knowing how the children felt about our new life, good or bad. I do know that it was hard for me.

A lot of learning was crammed into a comparatively short time. Meals seemed to be endless: the first early breakfast for the children and me, another for Warren around eleven, lunch for the children at noon. Sometimes everyone had dinner together, but other times it meant two evening meals as well. And then Warren would ask after the last one was over, "Would you like a little constructive criticism, dear?"

He couldn't be expected to think the food was delicious, but that was hard for me to take, believe me!

I didn't think the meals were so great either, but they were the best I could do.

***

Many years later, I was in the middle of my five years in Freudian analysis, and as my analyst was in Beverly Hills, this meant countless trips up and down the coast highway. Warren was a daily visitor to the racetracks, whichever one was open at the time, and the idea of a house closer to both of our activities made sense, so I bought a house in Beverly Hills.

My mother came to visit after my stepfather had died, and I recall something that happened on the day she was ready to take the train back to New Orleans. It was late on that midwinter afternoon, and the house was already full of slanting shadows from the low winter sun.

These shadows fell on my mother as she sat across the room from me, alone on the piano bench. She had come out from New Orleans to visit us, and to see her grandchildren as well. It was her first trip without her beloved second husband, and as I looked at her sitting there, alone, I found her a heartbreaking figure.

She wore a dark dress for the train trip back home, and one of the perky little hats she loved. This one was decorated with flowers, as they so often were, and the blossoms were the only light note. She looked forlorn and abandoned, and maybe a little frightened as well.

I sometimes wonder if it is possible for a mother and daughter to truly understand each other. The relationship is so close, and so much is expected of it, that it is hard to treat it as natural. Yet what can be more natural? It is a paradox, I think.

Sitting, making conversation in the late afternoon, waiting for the time for mother to call a taxi and go downtown to the station . . . alone . . . I wanted more than anything to go over to her, put my arms around her, and tell her that I loved her. But I couldn't do it.

Just as both Warren and I had been unwilling to alter our plans to go with her to the train station, put her on the train and wave goodbye to her as it pulled out of the station, so too was I unable to express any affection towards my mother. It is hard for me to recall, in retrospect, the cruelty I evidenced toward my mother on that day.

***

I remember Warren telling me, "He was my father, what else would you expect me to do?" In my astonishment of such a subservient attitude I immediately thought of a lot of things I would've done. What I would not have done would have been to accept such thoughtless authority as easily as Warren and his brother Alan did. Their father, Burton G. Tremaine, was an important man in the business world, on the financial board of General Electric for many years, and widely respected. He was credited with developing the concept of business parks, and his office was in NELA Park, Cleveland, Ohio. NELA stands for National Electric Lamp Association, and I've been told it was the first of its kind in the

United States and was headquarters for the administrative part of the giant General Electric Company. Warren's father and his partner had owned the Mazda Lamp Company which they sold to General Electric, becoming executives of the company.

His father was used to being obeyed, and automatically his young sons followed the pattern. They were perfect examples of "poor little rich boys," picked up at school by the family chauffeur, sitting, shivering, but uncomplaining in the back seat of the big black car outside their father's office, waiting anxiously long past dark for their father to recall their presence and give the order for them to be driven home should he still be occupied in his meeting.

Many years later Warren, when disciplining his daughters, would be asked by one of them, "Why, Daddy? Why do we have to do it your way?"

"Because I'm your father," would be Warren's invariable answer, "and because I say so."

By this time the new generation was hardly conditioned to accept such tyrannical commands, and it can be imagined that we had some noisy scenes. They often ended with Warren saying, "All right, Katy, go to your room." This was like a family joke, so much so that a young friend of our daughters, who often had dinner with us, told me years later that he used to make bets with himself as to how far through the meal Katy would get before she'd have to leave.

It was always Katy who was sent from the table, and looking back, I see that as a clear demonstration of the differences between my two daughters' personalities.

Diana, the elder of the two by two-and-a-half years, always accepted with apparent tranquility whatever the situation demanded. Katy, on the other hand, would rebel and argue and be sent from the table. I related more to Katy's behavior than to Diana's. Diana, incidentally, always ended up doing exactly as she intended, regardless of her pleasant-seeming acquiescence

Warren's father died as he had lived for many years in Cleveland, Ohio. His three living sons, Warren, his brother Burton, and Carl, the oldest of all, all took turns in being with their father during his terminal illness. Each of the brothers would spend one month to six weeks with their father in Cleveland. Warren and I lived in Santa Barbara, Carl in West Los Angeles, and Burton divided his time between an apartment on Park Avenue in New York and his farm in Connecticut.

Warren described to me the manner in which his father spent his last weeks on this planet. He was somnolent most of the time, if not totally in a coma. However, every afternoon around five o'clock, father Tremaine would rouse himself. He would open his eyes, and addressing whichever of his sons was in the room would ask, "What did the market do today, son?" He would then ask for the *Wall Street Journal* and his pipe, and when it was handed to him filled, would have a few puffs and an expression of pleasure would come over his face. He would comment on the market, glance at the headlines on the paper, and shortly thereafter, would hand his pipe to his son, put down the paper, and slip back into a semi-comatose state.

***

As my life with Warren went on, I found it increasingly difficult to express loving feelings. During the early years of our marriage I would sometimes ask him if he could tell me he loved me occasionally. Invariably he had the same reply: "Why should I tell you I love you? I wouldn't stay with you if I didn't love you." And with that I had to be content.

One of the lessons I have learned is the absolute necessity of having an object on which to focus one's love. It can be another person, a dog or cat, perhaps, maybe a chicken, even a plant . . . something we can exchange with. For instance, caring for a plant, one is rewarded by its growth, flowering, even perhaps by a fragrance. Whatever the exchange, we humans need it.

A friend of mine who delivers Meals on Wheels to low-income shut-ins tells me of the great difference in the emotional state of her friends between those with a pet and those without this kind of companionship.

Imagine how I feel even now, years later, that I was unable to show my mother my love for her. Because of that memory of my failure to act, I have on many occasions advised friends to share their loving feelings with those they love. Do it, show it, express it while you can.

CHAPTER TEN

Montecito Lifestyle

never enough time
for playing...drinking
where shall we have lunch?

"I DON'T HATE HIM; I hate what happens to you when you are with him." Warren and I were talking about Lou Soles, the genial owner of Susie's Beach, where many a memorable Montecito event occurred. Montecito is a beautiful green adjunct to Santa Barbara with a preponderance of affluent residents and one of the world's most attractive coastlines.

Susie's Beach, a small part of the coast, was so named because of the owner's black Lab. The dog loved swimming out to investigate one particular seal generally found cruising about not far off shore. It wasn't at all unusual to look around and see the seal as your swimming companion, its round wet head and its round dark eyes inspecting you curiously.

Lou and Dawn, his second wife, were great party givers, and during the years of their marriage they spent their lives doing just that. Lou inherited a considerable fortune, and thus armored against the world, as were most of our Montecito friends, including my husband and myself, there was no reason not to enjoy the beach, the sea, and sun. This was how many of us lived what became known as the "Montecito Lifestyle."

I'm writing now about the late 'thirties and 'forties, before and during the second World War, when our peaceful scene seemed a cruel contrast with what was happening in the real world. Some of the men were stock brokers, doctors, lawyers, and they of course had offices that claimed their attention, but the visitors from many parts of the world were vacationing and therefore free to be among the prime party goers and beach loungers. And why not? The beach was waiting, the drinks were free, the company congenial, and the sun was shining on the blue Pacific.

Besides these more-or-less local people, there were the Europeans, quite a few of whom had fled their war-torn homelands to share our white beaches and peaceful ocean. Although Santa Barbara was shelled once, up the coast a little, by an alleged Japanese submarine, fortunately the harm was unnoticeable. It caused plenty of excitement among the volunteer plane spotters and was the source of a great deal of conversation, both on and off the beaches.

Looking back on that period in my life I find it almost impossible to envision, or even to believe, that I lived it. Montecito was the Land of the Lotus Eaters. We watched as, for the most part, our sons and daughters moved away to make their lives elsewhere. The town was pretty much run for the rich with service-oriented businesses providing one of the few sources of jobs. The explosion came only after the war ended when a restless, frustrated people commenced roving the land in search of a new life. Why not exchange a winter-plagued industrial city for sunshine and sea? And what more natural than to return to the places where the men had trained for war? Arizona, California, New Mexico, and Nevada were expected to absorb tens and hundreds of thousands of people seeking warmth and sunshine.

Needless to say, fortunes were made and lost in record time. Men with shallow wants and minds thought only of money to be made by developing the once-empty and healing desert. No zoning, not enough water, no consideration given to planning . . . just throw up some shacks, dig up some cactus, build a few golf courses, and advertize desert resort living! And people came in droves.

At the time I married Warren and went to live in Scottsdale, we could drive for miles without a billboard or a person, only magnificent deserts and seemingly endless purple mountain ranges piled up one beyond another. From my bedroom I could see the Superstition Mountains. Sixty miles to the east and northeast were the Mazatzelles, dominated by lofty Four Peaks and air so clear and unpolluted I thought sometimes I might see coyotes or javelinas frolicking on the slopes. I thought that was all the beauty I would ever need, but then there was Santa Barbara.

Santa Barbara lies on the lower slopes of the coastal range. In front of us the sometimes incredibly blue Pacific, the Channel Islands ringing us about, spectacularly colored flowers on shrubs, on vines, in pots, syca-mores and live oaks spreading their welcoming branches, and now, fifty odd years later, air so polluted that at times even the harbor isn't visible from my terrace, much less the islands.

***

"Rich or poor, it pays to have money." This was the motto on Susie's Beach, and was initially coined by the owner of the beach, one of Warren's drinking chums. Lou was an amiable man. After his wife's death, he married for the second time, a dynamic woman named Dawn, quite a lot younger than himself, and seemingly living just the life she had been created for. Days and nights on and around Susie's Beach were defined in terms of parties. Guests were never in short supply. The host greeted all comers with a beaming smile and an invitation to have a drink, no matter what the time of day, or night.

Lou believed in free enterprise, you could say, and his own lobster pots would be seen bobbing up and down in the sparkling blue Pacific Ocean in front of his house.

Every so often his chauffeur/handyman would row out and bring the contents back to shore. The beach-combers would all congratulate Lou, and assure him that no other lobsters could match the ones caught off Susie's Beach.

The pleasure that the rich take in getting some-thing for nothing is the identical syndrome that causes them to plan their "vacations." Vacations from what, I always wondered. If one lives a life of hedonistic idle-ness, a vacation is only being idle somewhere other than the usual environment. The air is different, the scenery ditto, the people the same, although they wear different clothes and faces. Ourselves we must take along wher-ever we go, so if we bore ourselves, if we find our lives dull, we will find them equally dull in Paris or Majorca. One beach resembles another remarkably, varying only in details. Some have black sand and others are soft sparkling white. The well-oiled, lithe bodies of the idle rich stroll about the terrain as if they owned it, and in a way, of course, they do.

This is a world where beauty is all important. No one wants to see ugly fat on a fashionable beach. Con-sequently fruit juice is the order of the morning, with martinis and rum drinks postponed until lunchtime and after.

Looking back on that period, I realize how often I was bored. I learned, however, to ask the right questions of my dinner partners so as to afford me the greatest amount of free time, so to speak. Sometimes it would be a simple, "How was your golf game today?" that would release me from the obligation of making conversation. "Do you think the Dodgers will win the pennant this year?" was another sure-fire opening ploy with certain men. Horses and horse racing were other popular sub-jects. Questions about them were often directed at me because Warren and I both bred and raced horses. Our stud farm was in Ireland, in lovely, green County Kildare, and we raised some good horses over the years. We raced them in Europe as well as in this country, and mostly of course in California, where we lived. Looking back on that long period of my life, I wonder how I endured it for so long. There were, of course, bright spots, and at the endless dinner parties I would be grateful whenever I got to sit beside one of them. Even if the talk were political, and I was the sole holder of what were clearly held to be my radical if not subversive views, I could still enjoy certain of my dinner partners and learn from their good minds and knowledge of subjects that were of interest to me.

Susie's Beach became the focal point for the jet set types who enjoyed Santa Barbara and arrived in summer time to join the locals. It was just exactly Warren's cup of tea, but equally not mine. Numerous Hollywood film people were frequent guests, actors, and also business people connected with the film industry. Jules and Doris Stein were there often, for example, as were Ray and Gwen Bolger, Joe Cotton and Lenore, many famous and fringe famous. But regardless of who was in attendance, the atmosphere seemed always to be party, party, party.

Ray Bolger, a really darling man, went in with me on a partnership horse. We discovered one night at a party that our birthdays were only a day or two apart, both Capricorns, and so we formed a stable. We called it the Capricorn Stable, and we designed separate colors from the ones Warren and I raced under. I was entrusted with choosing the horse and designing the colors, and had a lot of fun doing it, since Warren was, generally speaking, accustomed to running things connected with our horses. I bought a beautifully bred little mare in Kentucky, but alas, we never got her to the track. She couldn't be kept in sound condition, and when it became clear that she would never stand training, we sold her to a man who retired her to stud, where she subsequently produced one or two fair offspring.

Lou's second wife, Dawn, was a woman of tremendous energy. She was also very attractive, a young woman glowing with health and physical well-being. She was perfect for the years that she stayed with Lou on Susie's Beach. When she finally left, however, it was a real shock to the community. It was said that she simply gathered up her clothes and jewels in the middle of the night, slipped out of the house into a waiting car, and drove off to the next man she was to marry.

As I mentioned earlier, Susie's Beach was the summer spot for many guests from the San Francisco Bay area. From Marin County down through the Peninsula, the well-heeled came to lounge on the sand, sit at the bar, plunge into the sea, and, in general, enjoy this Santa Barbara that we who live here call Paradise. We welcomed them all, and together partied our way through the summer months. Warren and I did our share of entertaining also. Having grown up in New Orleans, another party town, I was used to the routine, although, at this point in my life, I shudder at the thought of planning for two or three hundred friends to be my guests.

We had some "quieter" film friends, too. Ronald and Benita Colman, part owners of the San Ysidro Ranch who lived there in their latter years, were good friends. We played croquet with them often, but what a boring game that is! Even with Ronnie Colman as a partner, it seemed endless. He was one of the most charming of men, and that voice like flowing maple syrup was enough to melt any female heart. Croquet with the Colmans was always relaxed, but with Min and Vincent Astor over in Arizona it was a different game. Vincent was a real pro and took the game entirely seriously. Playing a game as his partner was endless and nerve-wracking. Each shot was studied with a running commentary. He was thinking of the opponent's probable moves, my move, and did I think I could make the hoop from my position? I would tremblingly reply that I doubted it, thereby ensuring missing it. It never could have been called "fun" as far as I was concerned. I ask myself why I permitted myself to become involved in it, and my only answer would have to be that I was responding to the social situation. Besides which, I was half afraid of Vincent himself. He was a big man, rather impressive-looking, and his being Vincent Astor was also a bit daunting. I've seen him pass out at the dinner table, and seen him as well being charming and extremely interesting. His subjects were croquet and Ichthiology, and by asking the right questions he could be an interesting dinner partner.

I never envied Vincent's wife, who was one of the most delightful women I have known. Min and I were in the same boat when it came to our chosen mates. She was one of three sisters, famous beauties all, daughters of the internationally known brain surgeon in Boston, Dr. Cushing. One sister married William Paley of CBS fame, another Elliot Roosevelt, and Mary, or Minnie as she was called, married Vincent Astor. I used to be impressed by well-known names, names that had been carried by men and women who played significant parts in the making of this country, but over the years I have come to recognize them all as human beings, all with weaknesses to overcome, all with hopes and dreams just like ours, like mine, like everyone's, and now I see them differently.

Warren loved the game of croquet and by nature was more suited to it than I. Patience has never been my strong suit, and the "strategy conferences" that took place after each shot were only to be endured as best I could.

I am writing of the tone of our lives in the fifties and sixties in Montecito. At home I always had things to do in the morning before Warren arose, but on trips, in hotels, I often read in our sitting room while he slept, or I might take a short stroll around the hotel, within a few blocks, but never far away. I was aware that when Warren did appear we would have a light lunch, and then we would drive out to the racetrack in whatever city we were in. On occasion the track was out of town, so we would leave in late morning to be there for the first race. In the main, that is how our days were passed.

Ruth and Walter Pidgeon were good friends, too, but not a part of the Susie's Beach crowd. They both liked Santa Barbara and came fairly often. I remember walking along Fifth Avenue in New York one afternoon with Walter, and asking him after the fourth or fifth time he was stopped by autograph seekers if it wasn't a nuisance. "No," replied Walter, "it will become a nuisance when people stop asking me for my autograph." The

Pidgeons were never a part of the drinking group; in fact I don't remember any of those involved with acting as being heavy drinkers. They were working people, and thus had responsibilities that the rest of us could avoid. I often felt during that time that I was fighting a losing battle, and the battle I meant was my husband's drinking.

I could have enjoyed Susie's Beach and the people there had I not had a constant apprehension about Warren and alcohol. Once he asked me how it was that I went to parties when he was out of town but never wanted to go with him. The answer, of course, was plain to me, but it was not to him. I have always loved dancing, and enjoyed good dancers, so that when I was at a dinner dance at the Valley Club or elsewhere, and the music was good, I had a wonderful time. I knew also that I wouldn't have to wait around for a husband unable to drive himself and me home, or leave him at the party for someone else to cope with.

Over the years I have learned more about alcohol and its affects. Now I realize that I was, in effect, more than just permitting Warren to continue with his life. I was "enabling" him in his alcoholism, as I would do for my son and my elder daughter as well. In plain terms, I was encouraging him in his sickness by staying with him, but I didn't know that at the time.

When I finally did leave my husband, in 1968, that culturally and politically tumultuous year, several people asked me if I didn't regret not having left years earlier. I had to answer that I hadn't been ready before, but that I did regret not having been ready some years earlier. But now, I no longer regret even that. I did what I was meant to do, I feel, and who knows how it would have turned out had I done differently.

I learned a lot during those early years in Montecito, but, ironically, one of the most important things I learned was the value of self-esteem. This is a subject that became very much in the public eye in the 1980s, particularly here in California. From my own observations and experiences, I can't overemphasize its importance. I'm not implying that people should become vain, only that they be comfortable and at ease with themselves—which unfortunately seems to be hard for many of us to achieve. I am more and more seeing children who appear to be totally at home in the universe, and this seems ideal to me. I have a feeling that those who become alcoholics, drug abusers, murderers, and who otherwise pollute the planet, do these things not only because they have no other resources, but also because they have grown into adulthood lacking true self-esteem.

Looking back, I believe that the saddest aspect of the Montecito Lifestyle was . . . and is . . . the waste of a life with its limitless opportunities for growth and expansion. Each of us who does grow, who does expand our horizons, is adding in our own way, however large or small, to the growth of humanity and to the entire universe.

Kit and Warren arriving in Honolulu on their honeymoon, 1936.

Kit and Warren honeymooning in Hawaii, 1936.

Kit in Scottsdale, Arizona, with unnamed home-bred filly, 1930s.

Kit with marlin, Guaymas, Mexico, 1938.

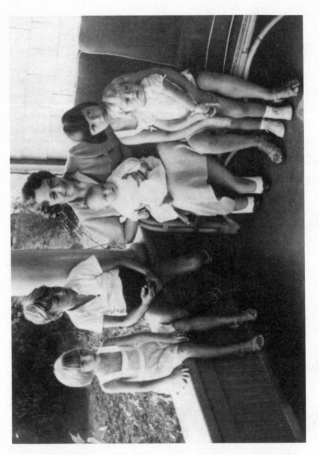

Kit's mother, Mrs. Charles Richard Frederickson, with five grandchildren, San Ysidro Ranch, Montecito, 1939. Left to right: Phoebe Giles Williams, Kit's son, Theodore Middleton Simmons, Jr., Kit's mother with Valerie Chase Williams on her lap, Anne Williams, and Diana Tremaine, Kit's elder daughter. Kit's younger daughter, Katy Tremaine, had not yet been born.

Teddy in uniform during Korean War, early 1950s.

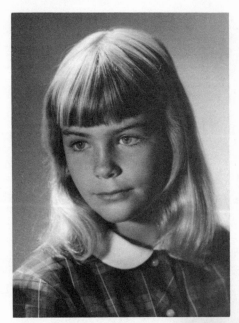

Katy Tremaine

Diana Tremaine

Kit on fence with Warren and Boss Chilson, Little Springs, Arizona.

Big party, one of many, at Kit's brother's house in New Orleans. Left to right: Betty Mickam, sister to Margaret Williams, who stands between Kit's brother and Kit, 1950s.

Katy as Diana's maid of honor, 1957.

Diana marries Sam Dabney, late 1957.

Kit Tremaine in the days when she still smoked and wore jewelry, at a fish market on the Bosporus in Turkey, early 1960s.

Kit with Richard Parker at Denny Ferry's 400-year-old farmhouse in Provence, France, early 1981.

Kit Tremaine in airport in Managua, Nicaragua, 1982, on a trip organized and accompanied by Blase Bonpane of Office of the Americas.

Kit on Coyote Road, Santa Barbara, 1980s.
(Photo by Fred Kenyon)

Kit in 1987.
(Photo by
Kevin Barry
McKiernan)

CHAPTER ELEVEN

Leaving

I turn my back
I walk away

IT WAS HARD FOR ME TO LEAVE WARREN. Over the years I tried, each time returning after a few weeks. But when I at last made the decision to do so, it was effortless.

By now I had made a new friend, Selden Spaulding, a Santa Barbara painter, and through him I rented a tiny beach house belonging to a cousin of his for the winter months. After thirty years of a life that had become increasingly confining to me, and in which I was miserable a great deal of the time, it was wonderful to be free. It felt as if a huge weight had been lifted from my shoulders.

When I was alone at night I would go down to the water's edge, where the Pacific Ocean spends its final energy on the warm beaches of southern California, and let the little wavelets wash over my feet. I would look up at the sky at the myriads of stars and planets, and rejoice in knowing that they were mine . . . my stars, my planets, my cosmos . . . they all belonged to me. It was an intoxicating realization and I began to blossom immediately.

I continued to see my two daughters, both living at the time in Santa Barbara, and kept contact with my son in San Juan Capistrano by telephone. I also began to meet other people and to make new friends. As my horizons broadened, so too did my learning. It was heartening to be among friends who shared my own interests and convictions, and life for me was new each day.

My interests were as they always had been, and now, with my new-found freedom, I was able to really expand. I continued volunteering at Democratic headquarters and continued also to demonstrate against the Vietnam War on Wednesdays in front of the Santa Barbara Art Museum. Our protest consisted of a silent vigil for the hour between noon and one, with some of us holding banners and others simply being there.

My involvement with the anti-war protesters came about because of a group of American Nazis from Orange County who came to Santa Barbara in the fall of 1969. While working at Democratic headquarters one day, a colleague and I went outside to better hear the message of their loudspeaker blaring from a black van passing the building. The driver, microphone in hand, was snarling out his views against "those Commie nigger lovers in front of the Art Museum." I was so offended by this that I told my co-worker that next Wednesday I was going to join the "Commie nigger lovers." That began my involvement with and commitment to the anti-war movement.

In the beginning people would drive by shouting obscenities and suggesting that we go back to Vietnam. Old friends were hard put to know what to do with us. I was at the time on the Art Museum's board of trustees, as was Selden, and it was interesting to see how those particular colleagues of ours handled the situation. Some would bow slightly, acknowledging our presence, while others simply looked away from us, preferring not to meet our eyes. Most of the people I knew during my married life were right-wing pro-Vietnam War Republicans, while I was the opposite. Warren pointed out to me one day that if America were to formally declare war on Vietnam, I would be known as a traitor.

Through my anti-war activity I already had met numerous others who felt as I did, and a wonderful spirit of comradeship developed. It was good to stand on the sidewalk with those I felt were my brothers and sisters, a totally new experience for me. We were ready to defend our beliefs and that made for strong friendships.

The first week I joined the demonstrators was the famous second visit of the Nazis. This time there had been much publicity. Television crews were stationed in second-story windows in nearby buildings so as to have good views of the action. Plainclothes policemen were scattered about the area, as well as uniformed police. We were told that the men in the upper windows were armed with machine guns. There was a tremendous tension in the air that day. So many people had swarmed into the limited space we were permitted to occupy in front of the museum that there was almost a social air to the gathering.

What followed was dramatic, and thankfully, brief. At twelve-thirty a stationwagon rounded the corner and pulled up at the curb. Four men emerged, all dressed alike in military uniforms, complete with highly polished leather boots. They came to attention, two and two, clicked their heels, shouted "Heil Hitler," and began their march up and down the sidewalk in front of us. They marched a few yards only, clicked heels, shouted the sacred name, turned to march back, then repeated their performance. Up and down they marched for perhaps fifteen or twenty minutes, then, as abruptly as they had begun, they got back into their car and drove away.

I confess to having been nervous often during my first weeks on the sidewalk. But as time wore on I became accustomed to being so visible. I had always been a private person, and in the beginning I always stood in the second row, behind someone else. I only finally moved myself into the front line when my cousin Anne, who generally stood in front of me thereby giving me a certain amount of anonymity, was obliged one day to leave before the hour was over. There didn't seem much choice for me except to step forward and occupy her space, so I took a deep breath and did it.

In my new life—from socialite to social activist—I no longer was obliged to defend myself for my political beliefs. With this realization I began to relax and take enormous pleasure in being with people who thought as I did. My new friends drank an occasional glass of wine, but wonder of wonders, they didn't get drunk and make fools of themselves night after night. And, I could always count on my "date" to drive me home.

I remember now that when I told Warren that I had taken a house and would move the following week, his only comment was actually a question: "Have you considered how you'll pay your income tax when you're single?" I replied that I hadn't given it any thought, but that I felt sure I could handle it. I also thanked him for making me feel so loved and cherished.

***

So it was that I moved down to the beach and began living. The friends I now saw were the friends I wanted to see. I made myself a promise that I would never again waste my time with people in whom I had no interest.

The only sad thing for me at that time was my growing realization that my elder daughter, Diana, was becoming an alcoholic. Perhaps she had been for some time, but for me the terrible knowledge was new and caused me great distress.

That winter of 1969 was a catastrophic one for Santa Barbara. There was a tragic oil spill right off the shore with dead birds, dead seal pups, many kinds of sea life piled up on the sand, and oil so thick on the beach that it was literally impossible to walk on it. This was bad enough, but to cap it off, right after the first of the year the rains came in unheard-of amounts; and torn loose from the mountains came huge boulders, trees, even old furniture that the floods had gathered on their way down. Flotsam and jetsam of every sort, size, and quantity imaginable came streaming from the hills, and all of these objects were added to the thick oil lumps covering the beaches.

On one of the days of the heaviest rain, my car was trapped in the garage, standing water preventing it from getting out and up the hill directly behind the house. Diana and her husband lived on the beach also, a mile or two from where I was, so I called and asked if I could take refuge with them for a day or two. Jim Keeny, my son-in-law, came down and checked out the fridge and such things, to be sure they were disconnected and would not short circuit in the event the water came in under the door. He invited me to come down when I wanted, so I gathered up a few overnight things, some extra rubber boots to share if I saw a needy beach dweller, tucked my little poodle under one arm, and started off walking down the railroad track. Almost immediately I met a man who wanted the boots, which lightened my load, and I continued on my way.

Later on that afternoon Diana and I decided we would make bread, but as neither of us had done it for quite some time, we made a loaf so heavy that if it had dropped on our toes they would have been broken. We had some good laughs while I stayed for a night or two with them to let the water dissipate enough for me to get into my garage. During my stay, Diana seemed entirely in control of her drinking, which gave me a temporary feeling of relief. I liked Jim a lot except when he was drinking, but then I could say that about many of the people I knew.

***

As difficult as it had been to actually take the step and move out of our house, it proved to be exactly the right thing to do. While making up my mind, I discussed it with a friend who warned me that whereas I knew what life with Warren was like, I didn't know what it would be like to be alone, and that I might be lonely and bored. Lonely and bored! It was exactly the opposite. I had been lonely and bored in my marriage, without realizing it, and I now experienced the wonderful feeling of days with never enough time to do all that I wanted to do.

More than once I have seen a formerly inconsolable widow or divorcee transformed into a busy, independent woman living a full and seemingly satisfying life alone.

For me it was the beginning of learning who I am and what I am all about. I was finding my place in the universe and realizing what I am to do for the rest of the time I am to be on this planet in this life. In short, I took the next few steps along my path that have led me from being a woman who thought nothing of spending thousands on clothes each year, including little nothings known as nightgowns that sometimes cost as much as two hundred dollars, to a jeans-clad political and social activist, to where I now stand, a serious spiritual seeker. I feel poised for the step to follow, which an astrologer friend recently told me would be through the door marked "out."

Among the new friends I was to meet and become close to were Daniel Lentz, now an internationally known composer of classical avant garde music and a fabulous chef besides. His wife Marlene and his friends Karen and Wolfgang Storchle became my friends as well. At the time I was chairing the Exhibitions and Acquisitions Committee of the Santa Barbara Museum of Art, and Karen, secretary to the Director, became my secretary as well for those meetings. She subsequently came to work for me as a private secretary when she left the museum and as a consequence we became good friends. I met her husband, Wolf, a multi-talented man, through exhibitions at Esther Bear's Gallery as well as at various museum activities.

Esther's gallery was THE gallery in Santa Barbara during the 60's and 70's, and an opening on a Sunday afternoon was certain to be a success as well as an opportunity to see many friends. I remember one such afternoon watching Wolf as he sat on the ground assembling his piece, consisting of many small rock elements . . . watching him and thinking how dynamic he was. He used to tell me that we had been sweethearts in former lives, and I believe that he must have been right. There was no question that a strong bond existed between us.

Wolf was killed in a car accident in Santa Fe, New Mexico. When his . . . by then ex-wife, Karen . . . called to tell me that he was dead, I said immediately, "He killed himself, didn't he?" and was surprised to hear it had not been that way. As I was in San Francisco when she reached me, I offered to call Dan, they being each other's best friend, and when I told him that Wolf was gone, he said the identical words I had used. We both loved him, and one of the most beautiful of Daniel's works is his requiem for Wolf. Both of us had been recipients of extraordinary letters from him during a prolonged and lonely stay he had in Mexico and for some reason I had destroyed mine. Looking back, I think they may have been too heavy for us to want to keep, indeed he became for me a companion. Wolfgang was an artist, a painter, a sculptor, a creator of multi-media pieces, a musician, a mystic, and a drug-driven man, and besides all his talent he looked like a young, blond, Greek god. I miss him still.

My own experimentation with drugs lies in my past and took place shortly after I had left my husband. I had been wanting to try LSD and finally the opportunity came along. A young Chinese-American student at the university in Santa Barbara gave me the capsule. I knew him from being myself involved in radical politics as was he, so when he presented me with a grubby looking piece of pink kleenex, as we were having lunch, I knew what it must be. I asked him somewhat hesitantly, as I didn't want to hurt his feelings, if it was good quality, as I was a little afraid of the procedure and certainly didn't want to add to the risk by taking inferior stuff. He reassured me, and both he and the other young man he was with offered to be with me when I took it. I thanked them but declined as I already knew who my companion would be.

I had no intimation that my entire being was to be changed on that bright January afternoon in 1969. Taking the LSD set my feet firmly on my spiritual path, and I was making progress along it. My most illuminating realization was the knowing that love alone was important. I kept saying, "All my life I have been intellectualizing and that's not where it's at. Love is the only thing that matters."

My whole being was filled with this revelation, and I have tried ever since to live demonstrating this truth in all ways that I can. I cried a lot during the afternoon. I found that music annoyed rather than pleased me. I had thought I'd want to walk outdoors and enjoy an expanded view of nature, but the light was so blinding that I soon returned indoors. I went in that house one person, and came out a wholly different one a few hours later.

There were other men in my life at that time, very disparate types, and I had fun enjoying my new-found freedom. In a very real way I was sowing my wild oats, which I had never done when I was young. Now I was unmarried, my grown children had gone their own ways, and I had no chains around me.

I took long beach walks, drove up into the mountains for picnics, went to foreign films, had long conversations with intelligent men, all the things I had always sought and not found in my previous life. I dressed as I pleased in jeans and sweaters and still do. I have never had a cocktail or any other hard liquor since leaving Warren. There was no need for it. I didn't have to go to late parties, long dinners, endless standing around, glass in hand at cocktail parties, my high heels sinking into the freshly watered lawns while I made light conversation with people I cared nothing about and who cared nothing about me. It was all behind me and now, at last, I could make my own choices.

CHAPTER TWELVE

Sunflower

Sunflower. . .
symbol of hope
I use money
freely

SOME YEARS AGO I was advised to start a foundation as a means of using my inherited wealth intelligently. I liked the idea and began thinking about the possibilities: who would direct it, who would know about how and where it should be distributed, how much would I be able to put into it and so on. I decided to call it the Sunflower Foundation. At just about that time, W.H. Ferry, a man I knew only slightly, came into my thoughts, and, as he was considering a life change, I was inspired to ask if he would become Sunflower's director. Ping Ferry, as he was called, turned out to be exactly the right man for starting my infant project. He had been a journalist for some years before becoming involved in the foundation world, and thus he was to introduce me to a new experience and indeed a new world. His more recent years had been spent as a fellow of the Center for the Study of Demo-

172

cratic Institutions in Santa Barbara, and from that base he came to me bringing a wealth of knowledge and his own life experience to enrich my life. He was exactly the right man for the infant Sunflower Foundation, which came into being with Ping Ferry at the controls.

Sunflower opened many new doors for me. I met people in worlds very different from my own and began to learn about the infinite variety of places where I would like my money to help . . . in short, setting up the Sunflower Foundation turned out to be one of my numerous landmark changes.

Looking back I see it now as a gradual change, gradual in terms of radical causes. My first director, while pointing me and the foundation in the right direction, did not open as many doors to the radical world as were to come my way later on. After a few years of pleasant friendship and learning for me, Ping left California to live in New York, and before he left, he suggested a young man we both knew, Richard Parker, as his replacement. Richard was pleased with my offer, we cemented the arrangement, and thus in the autumn of 1969 began what was to be a long and fruitful relationship which is ongoing to this day.

Richard wrote me a letter on October 16, 1989, addressed "To an old friend on our twentieth anniversary together." His letter accompanied a bound book of letters from some of the people whose organizations we have funded over the years. To say that I was touched would be an understatement. I was touched that he had remembered and noted our twentieth anniversary, which I, with a different mind set, had not done. Richard had contacted a hand-picked few of Sunflower grantees, asking them to write telling me of the many paths the money traveled and the ever-widening ripples it caused.

In his letter to me, Richard wrote: "I will never, ever forget the night I spent in Mexico City at a home that had been converted into a secret hospital for Guatemalans who had chosen to fight for their and their country's freedom. Nor the elderly black man in Mississippi who cried on meeting me, thanking Sunflower for helping the woodcutters' union that had brought dignity and a steady income to his family. . . ."

Here is the way one of these letters begins:

"Your support—starting in 1976 when few understood what PUBLIC MEDIA CENTER did, profoundly affected me individually and PMC institutionally," wrote Herb Gunther Chao, director of the San Francisco-based nonprofit media organization. "We realized for the first time through Sunflower's support that we were part of something bigger, connected to deeper values, to a broader community of conscience and commitment. Everything that followed for Public Media Center stemmed from that original vision you helped foster—powerful and clear—of cause and purpose."

My original intention for Sunflower was as a funder for causes not supported by the general public. Knowing that the funds available from Sunflower were relatively minor, it seemed best to give the invaluable helping hand to struggling activist organizations and I have never regretted this decision.

It gives me enormous pleasure to know that there are instances when our support has meant on-going viability for a group that has in turn been important to the planet. Richard and I did not always see eye to eye in selecting the agenda and it has been, in fact, only in recent years that he at last has been presenting me with agendas I approve. Richard, being very much the intellectual and very much the political enthusiast, tended to select projects involving dissemination of information, so that occasionally Sunflower's agenda would look like a list of publications: left-wing political magazines and papers, an occasional film, and so forth. But where were the so-called "hands-on" projects? I wanted to be involved with people. Yes, getting the information out was important, yes, that method might reach more people, but it wasn't what I wanted. The projects recommended by Richard were excellent ones always, and I do not regret those we funded. But the ones closest to my heart have always been projects where we communicated and assisted human beings directly.

For my part, I wanted to help people and causes such as those of the Asian women in the San Francisco Bay area, women who were cruelly exploited in the garment industry, Low Income Housing projects everywhere, which to this day are among the most desperate needs of the nation, and Jim Nollman's imaginative and valuable work in Interspecies Communication with different species of whales, to name a few. The list of community, political and spiritual organizations which have been assisted by the foundation is long and varied, and represents many, many individuals in this country and abroad. And it is a great feeling to know that through the Sunflower Foundation's grants, I have been able to help

effect change through these individuals and organizations over the past twenty years.

***

This morning as I was driving into town to meet a
friend for breakfast, the thought occurred to me that I
would do well to have someone with me who would say
to me, at least once daily, "Lighten up, Kit." This because
I was deep in thought as I drove, and thinking about the
plight of the miserable people all over the world, specif-
ically the homeless ones, increasingly prevalent in widely distributed countries around the globe.

One of the metaphysical beliefs I hold, one which
I have come to through reading, attending seminars, and
talking to a lot of people, is that we choose our circumstances, according to the lessons we need to learn. I
have been told by Indira, my spirit teacher who speaks
through the channel Verna Yater, that sympathy is not
necessarily always the correct approach to a problem.

As I drove, I passed by the little park on Cota Street
and looked for and saw several men sitting on the
benches in the barbecue area. I was reminded of the day
when passing the same place, I had seen a despondent,
weary-looking man walk slowly over to a bench, sit
down, and rest his elbows on the table in front of him.
My thought was, "Well, at least he has a table and bench
where he can rest." My next thought was how shocking
that I was grateful for the fact of the picnic benches being
there. It was cold and threatening rain that day, and I

wondered what shelter he was liable to have when the storm broke. And what kind of comfort was he getting from the bare wooden bench and table while he rested his feet and pondered the day ahead? And what kind of guilt was I experiencing to have those feelings about this man?

I asked Indira—who lived in India in the 1850s—if she would describe herself as a discarnate entity, to which she replied that she could be so described, but that she preferred to think of herself as "alive in spirit." This "alive in spirit" entity told me at our last session not long ago that I still had lessons to learn regarding stewardship, and suggested that I discuss this with certain people, and that I then write and publish a small pamphlet on the subject.

Being myself, as Indira would say, "one of the privileged ones," it can be assumed that I have given this subject much thought during my lifetime. I have written in my book, *The Butterfly Rises,* of my troubles in coming to terms with having been born into wealth, troubles certainly helped along by my childhood experience with a little girl who long ago chanted an innocent little chant about my grandfather being a millionaire as she was jumping rope. She doubtless meant no harm, but to my eight-year-old self, it was an indictment of me, and while I had no idea what a millionaire could be, it was pretty clear that it was something really bad. Add to this the small grandson of our cook, black as were most of the servants in the South, who spent a winter with us in our house and who was such a splendid playmate for my brother and me. He was however, mysteriously banned from coming into certain parts of our house—simply, as I was to find out, because he was black.

I believe that these two facts were probably responsible for my lifelong sense of social injustice with the resultant activism which has been so much a part of my life. Whatever the cause, I feel it a grace and am grateful for it.

CHAPTER THIRTEEN

John

John . . .
my love

RICHARD AND I SPENT A FEW WEEKS in the summer of 1981
with a friend in her 400-year-old farmhouse in southern
France. One day while driving around the countryside,
Richard brought up the possibility of our taking a house
together in Mexico for a few months the following
winter. I liked the idea, but as the summer wore on, the
political situation became more acute in the United
States, particularly in regards to our foreign policy in
Central America. With this in mind, I suggested that we
go instead to New Mexico, as I wanted to work with
some young friends of ours in Albuquerque. They were
heavily involved in Central American politics. He
agreed, and on the first of November 1981 we began our
tenancy in a rented, unfurnished house in Albuquerque.
The first few days we spent hunting furniture in rental
places and used-furniture stores. We ended up with a
fairly decent-looking house, thanks to some beautiful

old Navajo rugs I had brought with me. Thrown over chairs and sofas, these rugs transformed even the shabbiest furniture and gave a warm glow to the surroundings.

While Richard and I were still sharing the little house in Albuquerque, he and I and John Tomson, who had spent a couple of nights with us, drove east of Albuquerque trying to find a particular dirt road that Richard and I had discovered some time before, but we were unable to find it. The country was so built up now that it was difficult to find the less-traveled roads and we finally abandoned the project in favor of lunch at a restaurant we had noticed earlier.

This building was set well back from the main highway and the parking lot was jammed with cars. When we got in we understood why. The large, well-lighted dining room was packed with people, all in Sunday best, as if they had just come from church. Apparently on Sundays the restaurant advertised, "all the fried chicken you can eat," and the regulars came from miles around to avail themselves of the promise.

After waiting a few minutes we were seated at a round table near a window and proceeded to order and enjoy an excellent meal. I think I had begun to fall in love with John the afternoon that we met on the Hopi reservation and each subsequent meeting had increased my feeling for him. We had fun during the meal, laughed a lot, feeling each other out, so to speak, for although Richard and I were old friends, John was new to us, and we to him.

At one point when Richard and I were alone, John having excused himself, I told Richard that I would appreciate his leaving John and me alone for a bit when we got home, as I intended to "proposition" him. Richard laughed and agreed, so when we got back to our house he announced that he had more Christmas shopping to finish and was going out to a nearby bookstore, probably for a couple of hours. I reminded him that John had to catch a plane for Denver in the late afternoon. Richard went off happily, his idea of bliss being to spend time in bookstores, and John and I began a conversation while standing in the hall.

After a few minutes I gathered up my courage and asked John if he would like to go to bed with me.

He gave me a sweet smile and said no, that it wasn't the time, and besides, he continued, "Richard will be back soon." I thought not, but as we sat in the living room the front door opened and who should walk in but Richard. "Sorry guys, I forgot my wallet," he announced breezily, as he strode down the hall to his room. "See," said John, "I told you he'd be back."

As I sat talking to John, I remarked that it was surprising to me that I didn't feel embarrassed by his rejection of my invitation. Even at that early period in our relationship, I was already at ease with him, perfectly comfortable sitting and talking with him, feeling as if there had never been a time when we had not known each other. Later that afternoon we drove John to the airport, and Richard and I went to a Mexican place for dinner before going home to finish packing. Richard was

flying the following day to California to be with his
family, and I to Tucson where I would meet friends who
were flying from Santa Barbara to drive with me south
to Patagonia on the border with Mexico.

A few days later, when I was down at the ranch
where we were to spend the holidays in southern Arizona, I was not too surprised to be called away from the
breakfast table to take a phone call in the office of the
guest ranch where we were staying, from John.

"I have a feeling that a new lover is coming into my
life," I had said to my friend as I rose from the table to
go to the phone. And it was true. A new lover was
coming into my life, and I was about to embark on the
most exciting few weeks of my life. It was John, of course,
calling from Denver to tell me he was cutting his stay
there short and would be arriving back in Albuquerque
in a few days. I asked him if he planned to stay at my
house, as he formerly often stayed with a Hopi friend
who was living in Albuquerque, and my heart skipped a
beat when he replied that he hoped to do so. You could
have mistaken me for a teenager, I was so excited.

Our first night together we spent each in our own
room, but by the second day we abandoned all pretense
and John moved into my bedroom.

We had a wonderful few days together, and by the
time Richard returned from California John announced
that he was going to drive me back to Santa Barbara and
that there was no need for Richard to do so. I was
delighted, of course, and Richard made plans to return
directly to San Francisco. Our lease would be up in a
couple of weeks and, between working with my friends

at the Resource Center, enjoying both Richard and John, the days passed rapidly. I remember one night when John and I were alone in the house, having awakened around five o'clock, we decided to go out for breakfast. It was an icy cold morning, still dark when we got up, and the restaurant John wanted to go to was not yet open. He had spoken so enthusiastically about the extra-special sweet rolls at this campus-favored place that I was disappointed, but just being with him was so exciting that I was more than happy to go to a hotel restaurant and enjoy an excellent breakfast.

We had left the bed unmade and my bright red cashmere robe was thrown across it. John stopped in the doorway of our room and exclaimed how beautiful it looked. One of his characteristics was appreciation and I, in turn, appreciated his enjoyment of such things. In fact, during our short time together, I was often struck with the realization that "this is how it is between a man and a woman"—we laughed together, enjoyed the simple things of daily life, and of course, each other. Even in the earliest days of my marriage to Warren, I had not experienced this, and I thought it was fun.

***

When I finally did decide to leave Warren, I wasn't thinking about whether or not I would remarry. It never occurred to me that I would be unmarried for the rest of my life, and it's a surprise to me that I am. I don't know why it should be a surprise, but perhaps because I had been married since the age of nineteen and so I assumed

I would always be married. I've thought about it a lot and the only person who has ever mentioned marriage to me since my divorce, although I had it proposed to me a few times when I was married, was John. I would say I would think about it, because, truthfully, I was awfully reluctant to go back into a marriage.

In retrospect, marrying again would have been hard for me. And I am sure that, with John, my money played a part. He didn't have money, and although he was head of a foundation, they operated in a different way. They, he and his board, would conceive of a program and then go out and raise the money for it. One of their projects had been a highly successful program for the homeless of Denver. They had a large three-story building in the Skid Row section of the city. Different floors had differing rules. On the ground floor it was pretty much "anything goes," and the police were glad to have a place to take drunks and derelicts. On the second floor house rules were strict. There were mattresses on the cots, no bottles were permitted, no guns, no knives, and the atmosphere was quieter. In the basement a woodworking shop had been set up, and if any of the residents cared to, they would be paid a small stipend for work they did. It happened that John and a number of his friends all liked working with wood and they had developed a clientele where they could take and fill orders for furniture. The police chief and the mayor were both friends of John's and the police were only too glad to have a place where homeless men would be cared for on an emergency basis. A friend of the Foundation's was a doctor, who was available to provide medical care. As their success grew, there were two or three more doctors available to them, and a large staff of volunteers working at the center.

There were job counselors, psychiatric counselors. human-needs counselors, in other words, help in as many areas as possible, and the project was a tremendous success. At the end, John made a trip to Washington and returned to Denver with a three-year, five million dollar grant from HUD. This brought a lot of publicity, and the local AMA psychiatric group heard about the center for apparently the first time. They were astonished and decided that they should have the money as well as the facility. And that, apparently, is what happened. The AMA group visited the center, did not approve the facility, and in the end forced them out of the building and picked up the grant money. That is the way I heard the story.

An interesting piece of John's history was that his father had left his mother when he was two weeks old. And he spent his life, in a way, looking for his father, as I have, in a very different way, spent mine. When I met him in 1981, he had made arrangements to go to London that June to make a search for records of his father, who was an Englishman. John knew that his father had gone to South America to live—I've forgotten which country.

John and I drove back to Santa Barbara from Albuquerque, stopping for two days on the Hopi Reservation with our friends. We timed our trip to arrive at my Santa Barbara home in daylight, as John wanted to come to a new place that way. I loved the trip itself. We drove down side roads, stopped when we wanted to see some-

thing new, spent the night before arrival in San Berna-
dino and the next day, as we drove along the freeway,
John remarked that he could smell the ocean. Sure
enough, in a few miles we sighted it. We stopped in
Ventura and walked the length of its pier, had lunch
there, and arrived at my house in the early afternoon.

I had increasingly become aware that John was also
an alcoholic, but didn't want to admit it. A week after
we arrived, John drowned alone in the hot tub in the
little enclosed garden off my bedroom. I felt as if my life
had ended. But in the ensuing months I began to realize
that this death was a turning point, not for me alone,
but for his colleagues in his "catalyst" endeavors as well.
I know now without a doubt that I would not have come
as firmly along my spiritual way as I have without the
tragedy of John's death.

CHAPTER FOURTEEN

Kit and The New Age . . .

*a new way
of being*

I WAITED A BIT NERVOUSLY for Verna Yater in the tiny little room on Anacapa Street. Her office was in a small building across from the Catholic school, and we could hear the children's laughter from the school yard. It was 1982 and I was going to my first session with a woman who was a trance channeler. I was apprehensive, excited, and impatient, all at once.

It wasn't that I came to channeling entirely unprepared. Up to this time, I had experienced psychics operating in various ways, but none who went into trance as Verna did. By the time her door opened, and I was welcomed by Verna's smile, I was ready for whatever was to occur.

And what occurred was that I met and conversed with Indira Latari, a highly educated Hindu woman whose last incarnation had been in the nineteenth century. At that first meeting I was also introduced to Chief White Eagle, a Cherokee healer. These two entities have become my spirit teachers, and I have since learned a great deal from them. So much, in fact, that I cannot truthfully remember how much I knew about metaphysics before I began working with Verna.

The session began with a brief conversation with Verna. She was a woman in her mid-forties, very pretty with twinkling eyes and a charming manner. After greeting me she explained the process of channeling and told me I could expect to be addressed by Indira Latari. Verna described White Eagle to me as a Cherokee chief who generally spoke little, preferring to confine himself to a short greeting before giving healing sounds from the Angelic realms. Then Verna closed her eyes, and, after a few moments, appeared to sink into sleep.

Soon a rather high-pitched voice welcomed me and expressed pleasure in being with me. I was to come to know Indira's voice well, and to this day I smile when I first hear that greeting. Indira's welcome was followed immediately by some information rapidly spoken. When she finished, Indira told me that the information I was about to receive was not given to me alone, but rather for me to share with others.

First, Indira wanted to assure me that my intuition was to be trusted. Then she told me that all the answers I sought could be found within myself, as they occur naturally within each one of us. I have learned a great deal about the power of love, that love is the universal answer no matter what the question, and that we must seek to manifest it in all possible ways. As you recall, I had experimented some years prior to this meeting with LSD, and during the time I was under its influence that was the message I had received. My inner voices told me on that day that all my life I had been intellectualizing and that was not what mattered. The only thing that mattered was love. The further I have gone along in life, the more I have known the importance of this message. There is only one thing important in life . . . love, and there are untold ways to manifest it.

Indira has given me new insights concerning past lives, and I understand now why Native Americans and their philosophy of life are so readily acceptable to me. They gave me a feeling of coming home. I have been an Indian, both learned from them and taught them. I have been told of bits and pieces from my past lives, and am constantly learning how much I don't know. As an example, my eldest granddaughter was born with a handicapped arm. It happened that I was in New York during that winter, where my younger daughter was living. I was working with a yogi, and when I told him about the baby, he said that he and other yogis believe that we choose our incarnations in order to experience the lessons we most need to learn during our lifetime. Our parents, all of our circumstances, including the fact that our parents have to agree to our incarnating through them, and that, if this philosophy were correct, my granddaughter had chosen this handicap to further her progress along her karmic path.

It was the first time I had heard the law of karma spoken, and it made instant sense to me. Since then I have read much and conversed endlessly with others on spiritual subjects, as well as attending workshops and lectures on inter-related subjects. I have heard from

Indira and read in metaphysical books that after our evolving essence leaves our earthly bodies, i.e. immediately after our death, we are given an opportunity to review our lives in every aspect. From this review we are made aware of what we need to work on in our next life. It is thus that we know what we need to study and how best to learn.

At my second reading with Indira, she told me that, although the information I was being given through the channeling was confusing now, in six months it would all be "second nature" to me, and that, of course, has proven to be true.

I must say now that I have never equated the "New Age" with channeling, per se, nor do I equate "spirituality" with channeling, although I have gained considerable spiritual knowledge from this source. I agree with Ram Dass, among others, that it is not necessary to retreat from the workaday world to live a spiritual existence. In fact, to do that is impossible. You either live your life in as spiritual a manner as you are able, or you don't, but in either case your life must be lived as it is intended to be lived, and wherever it brings you, it is up to you to make of it the best you can.

I believe living a spiritual life means living according to the law of love, nothing more, nothing less. But that statement, simple though it sounds, means that we must realize love in all its manifestations and make every effort to demonstrate it at all times. It might even bring you to a job in a slaughterhouse, terrible though it would be to contemplate, as the taking of life is such an awesome responsibility, but whatever the work, it is your job to do it in as spiritual a manner as possible.

This, in fact, has been a real worry to me and a matter of conscience as well. I live in an adobe house, and at times my house is invaded by ants. I believe that they live in the adobe, and that when they are ready, they simply emerge. They swarm over the kitchen sink, over the washing machine and dryer, the floor, at times the walls, their busy little feet are everywhere while I go wild with frustration. So what do I do? I grab the nearest can of ant killer and spray everywhere I see traces of my unwanted guests. Laugh if you will, but I have talked to the ants, I have told them that if they stay outside they will be safe from my killing actions, but that if they insist on coming into my space, they must expect me to do my best to exterminate them. So where does that put me? Along with a lot of others who continue to work on themselves, even though it may seem hopeless.

Indira has her own way of entering into conversation with me. First she greets me, telling me how pleased she is to be once more meeting with me; then she goes immediately into the information she wants me to have. There have been times when I have brought questions of my own with me but never got to ask, as Indira answered them in her opening remarks. Other times, I would get so busy discussing the new information she had just given me that I would forget to ask her my prepared questions.

As an example, at our first session after my daughter Diana's death, Indira's opening remark to me before she invited me to ask questions was, "We wish to speak today of the one you call daughter, the one who has just passed over to our side." She then went on to talk about something that had been discussed between Diana and me during the last conversation we were ever to have on this plane.

Diana had telephoned me from northern California where she was living in a small town in the Napa Valley. I knew in the first instant that she was drunk, and after a minute or so I told her how hard it was for me to talk with her under the circumstances and that I would call her back in the morning. Diana denied, of course, that she had had even one drink, in spite of which I managed to persuade her that it was best for me to hang up, which I did. There was no disapproval in my voice or my words, only that it was too hard for me to continue the conversation at that time. I said to her, "Diana, all you want from me is for me to call you and tell you how wonderful you are, and I do think you are wonderful, but at the same time it is very hard for us to talk when you are drinking, so I will hang up now and call you in the morning." This occurred on the night before she died of alcoholism, and strangely, when I heard on the following day that she did indeed die on that very night, I had no sense of guilt. Rather I felt almost happy, if that word can be used in this context, that I had spoken as I did. I realized that it was the first time in her life that I had spoken the truth to my daughter on the subject of her alcoholism. I knew that it was alright between us and needed no explanation.

"We wish to speak today of the one you call daughter. She wants you to know that you are not to worry about the words that were spoken. She says that they were the truth."

It can be imagined that these words were very moving for me to hear. Not only did they confirm my own feeling, but they showed that there was still communication possible between us. Indira further told me that Diana had learned her lesson concerning her addiction and would never again have to bear that particular burden, and these were comforting words for me to hear.

On my dressing table there are two small Hopi jars. One of them holds two eagle feathers given me by an Indian friend, a sprig of white sage and a tiny pile of John's ashes. The other has in it two owl feathers, both given me by a dear friend of many years, as well as a porcupine quill, a gift from the same source. A similar small amount of Diana's ashes are in that jar and some time ago, I shook this little elemental pile of minerals into my hand and sat gazing at it and marveling about the biological miracle of life. I thought about the journey from the semen to the fetus, to the child, the adult, and now at last to these small bits of bone, of ash. Here was my darling first daughter, the source of much joy and companionship, here were all the pictures of her flashing through my mind, here in my hand lay what was now and forever all that was of Diana on this earthly plane and I sat looking and marveling as the tears flowed down my cheeks. And it's fitting, I thought, that love should end in renewal, that to return the ashes of the earthly body to the earth, or to the sea, is just as it should be and is assurance that there is no end to love. Love is in life, and in death and again in renewal of life.

I wrote a small prose/poem for Diana after she had gone in which I thought back to my honeymoon in Hawaii, where her life had begun. I wrote about the vast distance across the Pacific ocean between the island of Oahu and the west coast of this country where I live, about the soft, tropical days and nights, the pervading fragrances of the flower filled islands, and about the tragic and storm filled times of her forty odd years on this planet. Indira Latari, my teacher in spirit, has told me that Diana will not have to repeat this lesson in a future incarnation. She learned it in this life and I rejoice that this is so and that she chose to come into this round through Warren and me. I feel that by so doing she gave us the opportunity to help her take giant steps along her spiritual path.

I get the feeling that we've all learned a lot about loving ourselves and each other. When I am disappointed in myself I try to remember Indira's advice about loving ourselves. She tells us that we must learn to do that before we can learn to love and to know God, and that, as she says, is what we are sent here to do, and all else is extraneous. So I meditate and forgive myself then put it out of my mind. I don't say that this is easy . . . on the contrary, it is very hard, but it can be done.

***

There is said to be a universal fund of knowledge wherein all that has happened is stored and can readily be recovered. This source of information is known as the Akashic Record. I believe that there is a connection between the Akashic Record and Jung's theory of the collective unconscious, as well as the "Ring of Knowledge" encircling the planet referred to by Teilhard de Chardin. What fun it would be, for instance, to tap into it and listen to Socrates and Plato conversing on the steps of the Parthenon.

There have been times when Indira is ignorant of the information I seek, and says to me in a quiet way, "one moment please, while we seek the answer." After a slight pause, she then gives me the information. On other occasions when she is talking, she will hesitate, then say, "The channel's vocabulary does not contain the word we seek." And she will wait a minute before coming up with another word which will express her thought.

I am reminded now of the session my friend and editor, Steve Diamond, and I attended at the recording studio when Verna's colleague, Barbara Huss, channelled first the dolphins, then the whale. This awesome whale voice was speaking of the underwater damage done to the sea mammals by detonations and other man-made sounds. The whale explained that, no matter how much time passed after the event, the vibrations never stopped, and then went on to speak of the damage done to the entire oceanic system throughout the planet and to the living creatures in the sea. Barbara Huss transmits these sounds through telepathic communication with the cetaceans, then speaks these sounds in understandable English to us.

Indira has told me that she did not marry during her last incarnation. She lived her earthly life in the company of her father and left this plane in the middle of the nineteenth century. They lived in Jaipur, in northern India, and were, as she expressed it, "privileged people," with access to libraries, museums, and all kinds of research facilities. She and her father devoted their lives to exploring comparative religions and metaphysics, among other subjects. She was very much an intellectual and was happy in the life of study she shared with her father.

***

As a woman, the so-called New Age has proven most valuable for me. Despite the fact that we have still so much to learn, to know, it is a fact that we have had undreamed of opportunities opened up in the past twenty years. I have never been entirely sure of the meaning of the word "sin," but if I were trying to define it, I might say that to neglect to use the gifts given us at birth, to let our God-given talents lie dormant, undeveloped, that, in my opinion, is sinful.

Indira told me once that I have never had anyone to protect me. I realize that to be true and I realize also that I have gone through life seeking that protection.

In the course of the hours preceding John's death, we were having a private conversation and I had told him that I felt very safe with him. He kissed me saying that I would always be safe with him, but in a few hours he had died—and once again I was alone. The day after John died I walked around the house as if stunned saying over and over to myself, "It's not true, it didn't happen," and in the next breath, "But it is true, it did happen, I'll never see him again."

I am aware that the fact of having spent such a great part of my life alone has forced me, in a way, to develop my own strength. Neither of my marriages brought me the sense of security I needed. Quite the opposite, in fact, as both of my husbands were alcoholics, and thus had needs of security and love even greater, perhaps, than mine.

Octavio Paz, the great Mexican writer and poet wrote that man is the only creature who knows that he is alone. And it is true that we do have that awareness. There is no one to help us fight those inner battles, no one to even tell us how to go about fighting them, or to hold us in loving sympathy when our souls are desperate for comfort. We can be held in loving arms, to be sure, but the fact is that our own souls, our inner, higher selves, are still in there, inside of us, separate from that other one, no matter how strong the earthly ties between us. At least that is how it appears to me.

***

One day during a session with Verna, Indira said to me, "It is time for you to begin to teach."

"Alright," I replied, "what shall I teach, Indira?" "Teach what you know," was her answer. "And how shall

I go about beginning the teaching?," I then asked her.
"Speak to a few friends on your little machine,"(the
telephone) was her reply, "say that you will be at home
on such and such a day at such time as you wish, and
invite them for a cup of tea."

I followed her instructions and called five or six
friends. "If you are not busy on Saturday afternoon," I
began, "I'm inviting you to come over to my house at
two o'clock. I'll give you iced tea and store-bought
cookies and we'll talk. I don't know on what subject, or
for how long, two or three hours perhaps and I hope
you'll come."

Well, they did, and not only did they come here in
Santa Barbara, but also in New Mexico when I introduced a similar happening there. It was surprising for me
to see the eagerness of people for a forum where spiritual
topics were the cause for the meeting.

At the very first gatherings, as we came to call them,
the subjects were largely political, that being the chief
interest of those I had invited. Reagan was president
then, and was spending a fair amount of time at his ranch
in our neighborhood, so, one of our group being a
talented writer of limericks, she would produce one
relating to our discussion of the day, we would collect
enough money to pay for a political ad in the paper, sign
it "Neighbors of Reagan," to insure our meaning being
taken, and end up the meeting having had an enjoyable
time.

After meeting a few times, there was a subtle change
in the tone of the talk. Politics were largely ignored, and

one afternoon, when one of the participants introduced politics, I asked her to drop the subject as our gatherings were no longer a forum for politics. "Let's make them one," she suggested, and I was surprised to hear myself say "no." There had been a gradual altering of the mood, as well as of the subject matter, and a noticeable change in the guests. The political people no longer came, and those who did come brought guests, so soon we were borrowing chairs to accommodate three dozen or so human beings who all wanted to talk with each other and learn more about spiritual and metaphysical happenings.

These gatherings were enriching for all of us and I made some wonderful friends through them. My involvement and education in the world of spiritual knowledge not only hastened me along my own path of learning and growth, but through me, others as well. I think I can say that the past few years have been the most exciting of my life. My horizons are constantly expanding, and despite my energy level having been noticeably lower since my knee replacement in 1989, I still manage to go through those doors that keep opening before me and hopefully trust that I can continue to do so as long as I am in this degenerating body. In 84 years it has served me well, and I thank it even as I struggle at times to rise from a chair. It could be a lot worse.

As I grew up so in the shadow of my brother, I sometime wondered if I would ever contribute anything of lasting value to the planet, leave behind any contributions by which I would be remembered. I have, and I am very grateful to have been privileged to serve in such a way that I leave behind me a legacy of values that has been, and is, useful to others.

It is my hope that this book and my first one, *The Butterfly Rises*, will help in guiding others on their hard and often lonely paths. Every effort you can make to learn more about yourself will, in the long run, help someone else do the same.

CHAPTER FIFTEEN

One Rock...One Tree

to live
to learn
to seek
the future

I HAVE BOTH READ AND BEEN TOLD by my spirit guides that soon after our souls leave our material bodies there comes a period for each of us when we are asked to review our lives. Everything about ourselves, our thoughts, our deeds, our wishes, all must be reviewed, assessed.

Just as our earlier evaluations served to teach us what we most needed to learn, and thus to fashion the fabric of the lives we are experiencing at present, in this same manner we will re-evaluate what has gone before and so choose the path we next will seek.

When I was growing up in New Orleans, always under the shadow of my older brother, I would occasionally wonder if I would ever make any impression on the world. It seemed to me as if Laurence was so wise, so experienced, so much my superior, that I didn't see what I had, or would ever have, to offer of value.

My brother was my role model and I was always in
competition with him. I outshone my brother in athlet-
ics. I outran him, outjumped him over hurdles, rode
horseback, which he did not, played a team-worthy
game of basketball at school, played the piano, and
preferred spending my afternoons after school as high as
possible in the tops of the camphor trees which lined the
circle in the little park where we lived in New Orleans.
He had been gifted with a good mind, but so had I,
although I didn't recognize it then. I was in fact reluctant
to recognize my good points. But the real competition,
however, was for our mother's love, and in that arena he
was the winner.

So why was I so in awe of this not-so-superior
creature? Because it was what I was taught as a child. His
first arrest for drunken driving, to my knowledge, came
during the Christmas holidays of my debutante year. I
was shocked beyond words. Laurence was then an un-
dergraduate at Yale, and as New Haven was a long way
from New Orleans, he and I had less and less contact. I
realized that I hadn't the slightest idea of what he was
really like, of who he'd become since leaving home for
college, or, for that matter, even before leaving.

Then and later as our lives progressed, we were so
unlike one another that I often thought that we might
never have met had we not been siblings. Where Laurence was conventional, I was nonconformist. Where he
was timid, I was ready to take a risk. He was a city man,
an urban type, and I happiest in a country setting. I

needed space around me. I still remember Laurence's remark when he first came to Arizona to visit Warren and me. We were living on the desert near Scottsdale, and after he and Margaret had been there a couple of days, he looked about him saying, "Well, this is fine for you and Warren, I guess, but not for me. I need sidewalks." My mother felt the same way, and made a very similar remark on a similar occasion some years later. A fondness for city life was certainly one of the things they shared.

As for my father, I have literally no idea how Daddy felt on that subject or any other. Though I have deep regrets about never having established any communication with him, I realize it was because of his place in the family. I treated him as everyone else treated him.

He might as well not have been there, for all the attention he got. He was a gentle soul, with a damaged brain because of having contracted syphillis when a young man, and as such his importance in the whole family picture was diminished. He would be driven home from the office by the family chauffeur, come in the side entrance of the house, speak a pleasant greeting to whomever happened to be in that part of the house, and, holding in his hand the evening paper, would go on upstairs to his room to remain there, alone and unseen, until dinnertime when he would come back down and join us for cocktails. His death in the early '30s was a relief, since a burden had been lifted from me, but a tragedy at the same time as I never really knew him. In spite of the dysfunctional aspects of our family, the white-columned New Orleans house of my youth provided me with many happy memories.

In retrospect, I marvel at how different we all were. How strange that our karmic paths had brought us together to as a family, to work out, each in his or her own way, our uniquely individual needs.

***

Today I live in a house made of adobe bricks. We made the bricks from the soil on the very land the house stands on. When you look for it from down on the beach, it is invisible as it has become a part of the landscape. There was a time when I lived in a house with marble floors, and there were times when I enjoyed things I would no longer look at today.

We seem to go in cycles. I feel fortunate because for the past few years I have had a comfortable feeling that I am doing what I am supposed to be doing, and that I am doing it in the right place. My house, which I have created, nourishes me in a very real way, a spiritual way. One of the blessings I have enjoyed during my life is having been able to choose my dwelling places, and this one supports me and extends its warm welcome to all who come to it.

It is not large, but the openness of its design has an air of luxury in spite of that fact. Dark tile floors gleam below white walls, and the beams in the ceiling still have their bark. There are only a few rugs on the floor, and they are either Navajos or Berber from the Atlas mountains of Morocco. I have only old rugs, as I love the softness of their faded colors. It is a wonderfully harmonious house, and a day doesn't go by that I don't give thanks for it, and for the glories of the garden as well.

There is a small fish pond in one part of the patio, sheltered by two arms of the house, and the sounds of falling water from the little catch basin at one end are very soothing. It is at least four feet deep at the other end, which saves the fish, as otherwise they would long since have disappeared into the gullets of the raccoons and possums which come up at night to look for food. And believe it or not, as far as we are from the seashore, Great Blue herons surprise me from time to time. The herons will start circling above, then, if the coast is clear, they will land on the pond's edge. I go out if I happen to be home and, spotting the would-be predators, I'll jump up and down, wave my arms and shout "Go home herons, go home!" The noise and my actions frighten the birds, and they'll flap their huge wings and head for the bird refuge down by the beach.

Over the past decade, I have disposed of the majority of the art objects that I'd collected over a lifetime, and now the walls are hung with beautiful Indian blankets with here and there Indian artifacts radiating their spiritual values as well as their aesthetic beauty.

It's wonderful, and I am fortunate indeed to live in this part of Paradise. Live oaks dot the meadow-like land, cactus and succulents as well, this being a semi-arid climate, and just now bougainvillea is flashing wild color from the walls of the house.

Surrounded as I am by all this beauty, I awoke recently with a poem running through my head. I have not worked at poetry for some time because of concentrating on this book, but the concept and the title were immediately clear to me.

I have long since realized that as much as I appreciate the grace that has granted me this wealth of beauty with which I am surrounded, I no longer need it.

A picture came into my mind . . . a desert scene . . . almost bare of green. There are two objects, a medium-sized boulder and a tree. The sun blazes down and I see the rock changing its shape. It is the effect of the sun of course, changing the face of the rock with every small difference of its passage across the sky. I see the color of the rock altered by the same magic. It can never be the same from one split-second to the next. And furthermore, as it will never again have exactly this same configuration of sky and sun and shadow and cloud, this one rock is not only the totality of beauty, it is telling me a lot about the reality or non-reality of form.

Many things can be learned from this rock. How could I have thought its face was smooth? I now clearly see a ridge running along its top, a small ridge to be sure, but large enough to cast a shadow beneath it, and thus the face of the rock is changed. The color undergoes the same transformations. The surface under the ridge is now darker than the top where the sun is not obstructed in its radiating brilliance. This phenomenon is going to continue all through the day and night, day after day, month after month, regardless of season. And each changing aspect of the sky will change, however subtly, my rock. The moon's soft light works similar miracles, and I am aware that time, with the snows and the winds and the rains it must bring, will eventually destroy it in the end. But while it lives, I am content to live beside it.

My tree is one with widespread branches. An oak, perhaps a sycamore, a tree which offers shelter from the rain and sun. This tree shares with the rock an infinite variety of being. It too responds to the sun and the rain and the moonlight. The rising sun glistens from its shiny leaves, and if moisture has blessed it in the night, that tiny weight makes each leaf tremble just enough to shimmer slightly as the light breeze of early day blows through the morning. The leaves of the tree are notice-ably fuller in their growth on the south side and, when the sun is bright within the tree itself, it will be seen that some of the slighter branches have learned to lean that way.

At dawn with the coming of the sun, a special energy permeates the tree and the space surrounding it. It is as if it rises with the day, as if the sun, in rising from under the horizon, brings the tree up with it. The tree gives forth a strong male energy and as I lie, or sit, beneath its shelter, I am protected.

At midday the tree is still. Many birds roost quietly within its silence, but their presence will not be known until later in the afternoon. Then I will be aware of sound, bird songs, chirps, fluting melodies, practice runs and raucous squawks. The wings of the dove will whistle as they pass through the sky, the rustle of leaves, the bird calls from above, all of these delights will charm my senses once again. And when the sun of late afternoon begins its downward journey, its increased intensity will light up my tree like nothing man-made on this planet can accomplish. The tree will radiate light and it will be for me, as always, the object of my delight.

I see that this dream is, after all, a prose poem. It speaks to the distillation of my life, my joys, my needs, the changes that have occurred in me during the years of my life, and I will call it . . . one rock . . . one tree.